BUCKINGHAM PALACE

The
Diana
I Knew

∞

The Diana I Knew

*Loving Memories of the Friendship Between an American Mother
and Her Son's Nanny Who Became the Princess of Wales*

Mary Robertson

Cliff Street Books
An Imprint of HarperCollins*Publishers*

HarperCollins books may be purchased for educational,
business, or sales promotional use.
For information please write:
Special Markets Department,
HarperCollins Publishers, Inc.,
10 East 53rd Street,
New York, NY
10022.

FIRST EDITION

Designed by Joseph Rutt
ISBN 0–06–019201-1

98 99 00 01 02 ❖/RRD 10 9 8 7 6 5 4 3 2 1

To my wonderful family,
Pat, Patrick, and Caroline.

"And soul by soul and silently her shining bounds increase, and her ways are ways of gentleness and all her paths are peace."

From Diana's favorite hymn,
I Vow to Thee My Country
by Cecel Spring-Rice (1859–1918)

Acknowledgments

I wish to thank:

Freya Manston, the best agent a writer could wish for and a wonderful friend, for her unwavering faith in me and her constant encouragement.

Diane Reverand, my astute editor and the head of Cliff Street Books, for her sensitivity to my subject and her thoughtful editing.

Jane Friedman, the head of HarperCollins Publishers, for her enthusiasm and support.

David Flora and Krista Stroever of Cliff Street Books for their kindness and promptness in relaying messages and solving problems.

My darling husband, Pat, for his patience and support during the writing of this book and for his love and respect, always.

My marvelous children, Patrick and Caroline, for typing my manuscript on weekends and during school vacations.

My understanding mother, Hilja Baylor, for gladly forgiving the infrequent phone calls and many missed visits while I wrote this book.

My very good friend, Anne Dodd, for helping with the typing in the very early stages of this work.

John Katz, a professional writer and delightful friend, for explaining the whole process of writing and publishing a book.

∞

C H A P T E R

1

*W*hen my bedside telephone rang at two o'clock that Sunday morning, August 31, I knew it had to be bad news. I prayed the call was not about my son, Patrick, who had just left for his first year at college. I heard the familiar voice of my oldest friend, Judy Paine, say, "Mary, turn on your television right away. Diana's been killed in a car crash. It's the saddest thing you've ever seen."

I raced downstairs thinking, "My God, my God. That's impossible. Not Diana!" I turned on CNN and sat, tense and anxious, on the edge of the coffee table as the announcer repeated, "This is a breaking news story. The Princess of Wales has been killed in a car crash in Paris. This is how the BBC is conveying the news to the British public." The picture on my television was that of the British flag at half-mast with the words beneath it:

The Princess of Wales
1961–1997

I was stunned. I couldn't even breathe for a few moments. This *had* to be a mistake.

Following this image was a one-sentence written statement from the Queen and the Prince of Wales expressing their shock and distress at the tragic death. I couldn't believe it. The most famous woman in the world had died so suddenly—a heartbreaking loss for her admirers everywhere.

For us, this was a personal loss. Seventeen years earlier we had hired Diana as a happy young nanny, had attended her wedding, and had been friends ever since. I simply could not believe she was dead. I had not seen or heard the previous news reports of the accident. By the time I had turned on my television at two o'clock, it was eight o'clock Sunday morning in Paris. Diana had been pronounced dead at four o'clock Paris time. As I watched the live coverage, I couldn't even cry. I was feeling such shock and disbelief. A knot formed in my stomach when I saw the mangled wreckage of the blue Mercedes. No wonder there was only one survivor.

For hours I watched the live coverage, not able to turn away nor able to accept what I was seeing. To my left on a tabletop sat framed photographs of Diana with Patrick and with her own sons. Those visible reminders were wrenching. I finally fell asleep long after dawn, feeling numb with sorrow and praying for her young sons. If she had had any last conscious thoughts, they would have been of her boys. I hoped that she had not. The thought of leaving them would have been unbearable to her. I knew this because I had once faced the possibility of dying and leaving my own young children.

When I awoke late Sunday morning, I called my husband, Pat, and my fourteen-year-old daughter, Caroline, into our bedroom. They had slept through the night and had not heard the tragic news. I could barely choke out the words as I told them Diana had been killed in a car accident the previous night.

Their first reaction, like mine, was disbelief. Caroline's eyes filled with tears. Her first words were, "What about her children?" Pat, almost speechless with shock, felt as I did: "So young. So unnecessary."

My son, Patrick, was away on a freshman outing, so we were unable to reach him for three days. When he called, he spoke to his father since I was out of the house on an errand. Patrick, too, was shocked and grieved, but his main concern was for me. "This must be awful for Mom. How is she doing?" Pat replied, "She's having a very rough time. None of us can believe it."

The *Sunday New York Times* ran a last-minute obituary on August 31 that stated:

The royal couple had few common interests. Charles loved horses, his garden and traditional architecture; she loved buying clothes, listening to pop music on her Walkman and gossiping on the telephone.

I was furious, thinking, "How *dare* they make her sound so shallow!" I felt their observations were unkind and unfair to Diana and trivialized her as a person as well as her charitable efforts. My husband, Pat, suggested I write a letter to the editor describing our very different and very positive view of our former nanny.

The next day, Labor Day, I was sitting up in bed, mentally composing my letter to the *New York Times,* when a young researcher from ABC News, Michael Baltierra, called to ask if we would "consider participating" in a program about Diana. I requested that he call back in ten minutes while I discussed the idea with my husband. We had never talked about our relationship with Diana with anyone from the media because we felt that it was a private matter. However, my mother-in-law, of whom I am very fond, had given an interview to the *Houston Chronicle* just before the wedding in 1981, so the fact that Diana had been our nanny had appeared in the press at that time.

Pat and I decided that perhaps it was finally time to talk about Diana. The mean-spirited and critical comments about her in the media coverage and certain books had upset both of us. This was *not* the Diana we had known, and we wanted to help balance the record. With her untimely death, we felt she might have wished us to stand up for her now. We agreed to work with ABC that same afternoon.

A short ninety minutes later, Antonio Mora, a news correspondent, arrived with a camera crew at our home outside New York City to film our recollections of Diana. Our view of Diana as a warm and wonderful person must have been convincing. Antonio admitted that he hadn't followed Diana closely before, but really admired her now.

We did not anticipate the tremendous interest our Tuesday evening interview on *ABC World News Tonight* would generate. Our telephone started ringing within minutes of my spot, as Antonio had predicted. For the next two days, we were besieged with well over a hundred phone calls from network and cable television, local channels, magazines, and newspapers in the United States and Europe. Several reporters and photographers arrived at our front door without warning. We were glad that so many people wanted to hear a fresh and positive perspective on Diana. At the same time, the media frenzy gave us a taste of what being in the limelight is like. My husband said, "This is so overwhelming for us, can you *imagine* what Diana must have gone through year after year?"

Every reporter asked us if we were going to the funeral. Our regretful answer was that we had not received an invitation. We had learned from Floyd and Amanda Bradley, our friends in London, that the funeral was by invitation only and that the list was still under review. We never expected to be on the list. With Diana gone, who at the palace would think to include us? I never thought to call her private secretary in London. I'd completely forgotten that I had the number in my address book. Nor did it occur to me to contact the British consul general in New York City to ask if I could *please* have an invitation.

On Wednesday, September 3, I'd been awake at five in the morning for an interview with Charles Gibson on *Good Morning, America*. Apparently, I still hadn't accepted Diana's death because at the end of our talk Charles observed, "It's wonderful to hear you speaking about her in the present tense. Do you realize you've been doing that?" I hadn't been aware of this at all.

After I returned home that morning, our telephone rang incessantly with requests for interviews and photos. By midafternoon I was exhausted. At four o'clock I was reaching to disconnect the telephone when I answered one last call.

Thank heavens I did! I heard, "Mrs. Robertson? This is Ian Hamilton from the Lord Chamberlain's office."

I held my breath and prayed, "*Please* let this be the palace."

He continued: "We would like to invite you, your husband, and your son to attend the funeral of the Princess of Wales on Saturday in London." I was speechless. I could feel my heart thumping. I never thought to ask him how our name had been selected. Later, in London, I learned that the Spencer family had given instructions to review Diana's personal records, including her Christmas-card list, with the help of her closest aides.

"Yes, of course, we absolutely want to attend," I answered without hesitating. "Thank you *so* much. I can't tell you how much this means to me. I'll have to make travel plans on very short notice, so may I call you back to confirm? How late can I reach you?"

He replied, "Anytime. We're working twenty-four hours a day. But I need your reply within an hour." I jotted down his telephone and fax numbers and set about making travel arrangements.

My husband had just walked in the door, so we were able to discuss who would travel and how. Both children's passports had expired and could not be renewed in less than a day from the suburbs where we live. Caroline, our daughter, was starting at a new school the very next day. Pat felt he needed to stay home with her. "Besides," he said, "I cried at the wedding. I'd never make it through the funeral."

Though I dreaded the prospect of coping with the heartbreak of the funeral on my own, I felt I had to be there at the end, no matter what. We had been with Diana at the very beginning of the courtship. We had attended her wedding with tremendous joy. We had kept in touch ever since.

I had to say good-bye to her in person. I said to Pat, "We were there for the 'wedding of the century.' This will be 'the funeral of the century.' Yes, I have to go." Then we just looked at each other. We couldn't find any words to express the sorrow we both felt.

I called American Airlines, where we had frequent-flier miles, and frantically explained that I had to be in London by Friday evening, but did not say why. Surprisingly, the reservation clerk had seen me on television, recognized my name, and assured me she would get me on a flight.

I had been unable to reach the Bradleys, but could not wait any longer to call Mr. Hamilton back. After I explained that only I would be attending the funeral, he asked for a London address to which my admission card could be sent. I gave him the Bradleys' Chelsea address with the caveat that "I haven't been able to confirm this with them yet." Then I asked, "What should I do if I don't receive my card?"

"Don't worry," he reassured me. "Just come to the North Door. Your name will be on a list. By the way, the dress is dark clothing, hat optional. The doors open at 9:30 and everyone must be seated by 10:15. Don't be late."

The next thirty-six hours were a blur of fielding telephone calls, packing, making plans for my family during my absence, and calling the Bradleys in London to see if I could stay with them during what I knew would be a harrowing weekend. Whenever I had a moment to spare, I would think of Diana, cry quietly, and feel not only tremendous sadness but also real anger about her death. That car accident could have been prevented in so many different ways. The unfairness of it overwhelmed me. And then, of course, I would think of her boys—always of her children.

Friday morning, September 5, Pat and Caroline drove me to the airport to catch my flight to London. By then, I had spoken with the Bradleys, who had invited me to stay at their home in Chelsea. Floyd kindly insisted on meeting me at Gatwick Airport late Friday night. Floyd is a longtime friend of ours from graduate school twenty years ago. At least I would have some comfort and support in the absence of my own family.

During the seven-hour flight to London, I sat overwhelmed and exhausted, still unable to absorb the irrefutable fact of Diana's death. The previous week had seemed unreal—first, the sudden tragedy and then the unnerving media attention. Frequently during the trip I would feel tears welling up in my eyes. I desperately needed to have a good, long cry to relieve the grief inside, but I was wound up too tight to let go.

I simply could not believe that I was traveling to Diana's *funeral.* It seemed such a short time since Pat and I had traveled to her wedding with great joy and excitement. The contrast was agonizing. I turned my thoughts to my happy

and vivid memories of Diana and to the improbable circumstances that had linked my family to the beautiful and loving
Princess of Wales.

∞

*L*ooking back, I was struck by the random events that resulted in our moving to London in January of 1980 and needing a part-time nanny for that year. I've always been a believer in fate. My husband's company, Exxon, asked him to take a short-term assignment in London starting January 1. The previous fall I had returned to full-time work at The Morgan Bank after the birth of my son, Patrick, in May 1979. Although I adored my son, I had invested years of hard work and study in my career in finance. Also, we needed my salary to pay the bills. I had been lucky to find Chris Williams, a reliable, caring Jamaican woman who'd raised her own three children, to live in during the week. Chris was a gem, but privacy was a problem in our small three-bedroom house.

When Pat called me from London just before Thanksgiving, I was torn. I derived satisfaction and pride from my work, but I really disliked my boss at that time and I missed my child dreadfully. I thought living in London, my favorite city, would be wonderful, but I worried about the impact the move would have on my career. I discussed my options with Bill Setterstrom of the bank's personnel department. Bill had been in the navy and viewed family separations as fairly normal. At first, he suggested that I stay at my job in New York. I pointed out that Pat was not being assigned to a battleship at sea where I could not follow. "In fact," I said, "this is London, Bill, and I want to go!"

In the end, he offered me six months' leave of absence "to enjoy your new baby and living in London." Furthermore, if my husband were to stay in London, the bank would give me a job in England. If we came back to New York, I would return to The Morgan Bank there. This was a generous offer, especially in the early days of women officers at major banks. I am still profoundly grateful to Morgan for its flexibility and kindness.

My husband left on New Year's Day 1980 while I waited a week to close up our little house in Bronxville, a small suburb of New York City, and to settle last-minute domestic and financial matters. That week my delightful English neighbor, Rosie Finn, stopped by with dinner and some helpful advice. "If you find you need a nanny, be sure to call this agency. It's the one I and all my friends used." The name she wrote down was "Occasional and Permanent Nannies," located in

Beauchamp Place. I thanked her, but since we'd just finished with live-in help and wanted our privacy back, I did not foresee any need for a nanny in London. As it turned out, I never got my six-month holiday.

I was literally walking out the door with Patrick in my arms to leave for the airport when the telephone rang. It was Bill Setterstrom from the bank with a change of plan. "Mary, thank heavens I caught you in time. We'd like you to take a part-time job at our consortium bank in London. Call Freddie Vinton, the head of our office, as soon as you arrive." I was floored and asked if this was his idea of a joke. He snapped back, "No, it's not. I wouldn't be calling at six o'clock on a Friday night if this were a joke! Have a safe trip and call Freddie."

After our long flight, I was glad to see Pat waiting for us at Heathrow and very excited about living in London for the next six months. As soon as we were settled in the large but dreary flat my husband had rented for us, I dutifully called Mr. Vinton about my prospective job. Since I had managed to catch the flu as soon as I landed, Freddie interviewed me in my living room as I sniffled and coughed. I did not want a job at that point but felt I should not say no. The assignment sounded easy and flexible. I also wanted to stay in the bank's good graces. The job involved teaching American credit standards and procedures two days a week to trainees at the Saudi International Bank of which Morgan was a part owner. Consequently, I needed a nanny for those two days.

I had found a wonderful, mature, well-trained nanny, Mrs. Chapman, through a temporary baby-sitter agency Exxon used regularly, but Nanny Chapman had a sick husband and could not commit to a steady job. The few girls that same agency had sent were unsatisfactory. Meanwhile, I was becoming more and more anxious about turning my precious son over to any stranger in a large city where we knew virtually no one. Then I recalled my neighbor's enthusiastic recommendation and telephoned "Occasional and Permanent Nannies."

A woman with a well-bred accent answered, and I explained that I needed a nanny only two days a week, any two days. "Hmm," she replied, "that will be difficult. Most of our people want full-time work. Are you *sure* you don't want a full-time nanny or an au pair?"

"No," I said, "we've had full-time, live-in help and don't want that again." I was feeling very discouraged. I could hear her fingers ruffling through a Rolodex as she murmured, "Well, I'll see what we can do. . . ." She continued to flip briskly through the alphabet. "Oh, here's someone! Diana Spencer. She's available Mondays and Thursdays. Let's see what her references say." She paused as she read her file, then exclaimed, "Good heavens! She worked for friends of mine last summer. What did they have to say about her? Ah, sweet-tempered; good with children; willing to do whatever she's asked. How does that sound?"

I thought that sounded terrific. There was only one

condition. "She'll only work in SW1, 3, or 7." These are the most central and elegant zip codes in London. We were living in SW1 in a converted Georgian town house right in Belgrave Square, half a block from the Spanish embassy. Later that afternoon, the agency called to tell me they'd arranged an interview on Diana's next free day.

I've relived my first glimpse of that lovely child countless times since. At eleven o'clock that morning in early February, I heard the elevator door opposite our flat open and close. I answered the doorbell and there was Diana, the wintry sunlight falling on her from the skylight above the stairway to the left. She stood calmly her head slightly bowed, looking up at me through her bangs. She was lovely, with perfect English skin, a slight blush on her cheeks, and clear blue eyes. She simply glowed with youth and good health. She was dressed in a brown corduroy overall-type skirt, a turtleneck sweater, and long fuzzy socks with loafers. She wore a simple gold necklace with a capital letter *D* around her neck. She looked just like the suburban teenagers I had known in America, only ever so much prettier. I breathed a sigh of relief as she said, "Mrs. Robertson? I'm Diana Spencer. So nice to meet you."

At the time, I did not realize that her upper-class accent and flawless manners meant that this was no ordinary babysitter. Nor did I realize quite how young she was because she was so poised and graceful. I simply thought, "Thank heavens. Here's someone I could leave Patrick with." She was well dressed and well mannered. I assumed she came from a background like mine—a suburban home, good schools, and a father in business or a profession. Comfortable and secure, but nothing fancy.

We sat down to talk, facing each other on the lumpy orange print sofas in our toy-strewn living room. London rental flats come fully furnished, unlike American apartments. This flat did not reflect my taste in colors or furniture. Patrick crawled around the living room as she and I discussed her duties and hours. She reached down to ruffle his hair or hug him as we talked. He was a happy, appealing child, and her response to him was warm and spontaneous. I asked her why she wanted this job when she already worked at a kindergarten. Diana volunteered, "I adore working with children."

We agreed that she would work Mondays and Thursdays from nine-thirty to five-thirty for two pounds an hour, a little under five dollars an hour at the exchange rate in 1980—$2.20 to one English pound. She was to play with Patrick, feed him, read to him, take him out for walks, change diapers—the usual nanny chores. My only specific instructions were to keep him warm and dry and to guard him with her life when she took him out. I stressed, "Patrick is the most important thing in the world to me. You'll understand when you're a mother yourself."

During that first meeting, Diana set clear limits for herself. I asked if she would be available to baby-sit from time to time in the evenings or on weekends. Looking directly at me, Diana very politely said, "No, I prefer to keep my evenings and weekends free." She offered no apology or explanation. It would never have occurred to me to ask her why or to try to talk her out of her position. The tone of our relationship was set that first day. We genuinely liked each other and we also respected each other's privacy.

Interestingly, I never asked her directly for references. Her manners spoke for themselves, and the nanny agency had already looked into her previous work. They had mentioned that she worked at the Young England Kindergarten as well. I liked her and trusted her from the start, and she must have liked me and my child or she never would have stayed with us. The instinctive trust I felt for Diana was crucial. She and I would be sharing a very precious little being.

When I think about her now, it seems remarkable she ever came for an interview with an American family in a temporary flat—certainly she was accustomed to more elevated circles. I feel it says volumes about how unpretentious she was and how genuinely she loved working with children. Possibly, she was also curious about Americans or sought the anonymity working for a non-English family would provide.

Her first day with us was February 14, Valentine's Day, an easy day to remember. At the very beginning she was quiet, almost shy, with me. I would have described her as tenderhearted, polite, and good-natured, but rather serious underneath—not frivolous in any way or I would not have hired her. I wanted a nanny who would be solidly focused on my child as I headed off to my office at 99 Bishopsgate two days a week.

That first day I left Patrick with Diana only for short periods of time, to run to the grocery store or to do other errands, in order to observe them together for a while. I have always been cautious about my baby-sitters and have tested them out before leaving them alone with my children for longer periods. Patrick took to Diana immediately and gurgled happily as they played together. When I peeked into his bedroom from time to time, I had no qualms about her fondness for him.

Diana and I soon developed a very comfortable relationship. When she arrived in the morning, she would exclaim "Patrick!" and scoop him up in her arms for a cuddle. He'd smile cheerfully in response. Then she and I would chat about our respective plans for the day as I finished dressing. Patrick was always nearby, either crawling on the floor or snuggling in her arms.

Sometimes Diana and I would compare shopping tips. She especially liked Benetton and Harvey Nichols, a very chic department store in Knightsbridge. I thought London was so expensive back in 1980 that I bought nothing for myself, only toys and clothes for Patrick, and some antique pine furniture for our library at home.

Diana had budding fashion awareness even at eighteen.

One morning she remarked on my burgundy silk blouse, saying, "That's a very good color on you, Mrs. Robertson. You should wear it more often." And every time I've worn that color since, I've thought of Diana standing in my bedroom doorway with Patrick nestled on her hip.

Another morning she boosted my ego by commenting, "You're *so* much smarter than I am, Mrs. Robertson." She thought I was intelligent because I had graduated from a well-known college and the Harvard Business School and worked in "the City," the financial district of London. Good-naturedly, she would bemoan her own lack of higher education and career training. She had not achieved passing grades in any "O"-level exams. In the English system, "O" meant ordinary, while "A" levels were for university-bound students. She had returned home before completing her course at the finishing school in Switzerland she had attended after boarding school. By American standards, she barely had a high school education. I later learned this was quite normal for the daughters of the aristocracy.

At that time, Diana seemed quite unaware of her unerring instincts with regard to other people—her ability to understand their concerns and to communicate her caring directly and sincerely. I am sure she did not realize how appealing I found the combination of her genuine warmth with her natural refinement and modesty. I knew she was a lady, long before I learned of her position in life.

I learned about Diana and Patrick's daily activities

when I arrived home at five-thirty. I was always very prompt. I discovered that I physically craved coming home and hugging Patrick after eight hours away. I wondered how I'd survived those few months of full-time work back in Bronxville. I also felt Diana deserved a break after a long day with an active toddler. I could easily tell that they had both had a full and happy day. Patrick always looked cheerful and energetic when I returned, and they always hugged each other enthusiastically as Diana left. Then I held him as the door closed on our marvelous nanny.

Diana's routine with Patrick consisted of playtime on the floor with his toys and blocks—he loved to build—and lots of long walks in the fresh air. The English are mad for fresh air. She always greeted him with a cuddle in the morning and snuggled with him before saying good-bye in the evening. Clearly Diana has always had a tactile way of showing affection. She fed him breakfast and lunch, either baby food in jars from Boots, the chain pharmacy in England, or yogurt or scrambled eggs until he was able to chew. He seldom took a nap, so it was a long day requiring the patience, love, and stamina that Diana had in abundance.

Patrick loved to be read to from two English nursery-rhyme books that I'd purchased at the W. H. Smith bookshop in Sloane Square. At a friend's suggestion, I had established the early reading routine that Diana enthusiastically followed on her days with him. She would read or sing the rhymes to him and then ask him, "Where's the bunny?" or

"Where's the dog . . . tree . . . house . . . cat?" or whatever. He would give his wonderful smile and point to the correct figure on the page. She never tired of reading these two books to Patrick. He was an early reader and has always loved to read, thanks largely to this early experience.

My husband and I were thrilled when Patrick began to walk during the weekend of his first birthday in May. When Diana arrived on Monday morning, I announced the news of this major achievement. Diana gave Patrick an extra-big hug and told him how "very proud" she was of him. She and I were also pleased about Patrick's walking, because, as he became more mobile and active during the day, he took longer naps, which she and I greatly appreciated.

Besides her baby-sitting duties, Diana went out of her way to be helpful. Without my asking, she would wash up breakfast dishes or finish a batch of laundry. Since she had a car in London and I did not, she would sometimes pick up and deliver bulky diapers and baby food for Patrick when he and I were out. I would reimburse her the next time I saw her. She would leave the package at my apartment door with a brief note explaining that she hoped this would save me some trouble. Her note would be written on simple cream-colored engraved stationery. At the time, it didn't seem unusual to me that a teenager would have such elegant paper or would use it for household notes. I still had my own engraved stationery purchased at Tiffany as a real splurge years ago.

As the weather grew warmer, I asked Diana to take Patrick to buy a spring jacket. I thought she would enjoy shopping for him and gave her the money in advance. On her own, she chose a bright yellow windbreaker with a hood for warmth in case of cool breezes. We have the most wonderful picture of Patrick smiling out at the world with his face framed by the yellow hood. Another day Diana brought along a yellow rubber duck as a present for Patrick's bathtime. This has, of course, become a family treasure and has moved everywhere we've lived since.

The Belgrave Square flat was centrally located and ideal for people with small children. The flat came with a key to the large private garden in the center of the square and was a fifteen-minute walk to Hyde Park and Saint James's Park—great for airing babies in strollers or toddlers learning to walk. On rainy days Patrick and I could visit Westminster Abbey or the National Gallery for a leisurely browse.

Neither Diana nor I liked the flat itself, though she was a good sport about its shortcomings. A temporary executive rental, the flat suffered from a lack of sunlight and a depressing color scheme with lots of brown—not a place in which one wanted to spend long hours in the daytime as Diana and I did. The building was anything but homey, as the Royal Automobile Club occupied the first three floors of the former town house and a noisy bachelor lived above us on the fifth floor. The elevator was constantly broken, so

Diana and I had to carry Patrick, a solid twenty pounds at age one, his stroller, and often packages up the three long flights of stairs on a regular basis. In addition, the bathtub upstairs had begun to leak steadily into the main bathroom in our flat, which meant Diana and I did a lot of mopping up.

In 1980 Diana was a happy, well-adjusted, slightly plump young woman with a healthy appetite. I know this because I could tell from my fridge what she'd eaten for lunch each day. Neither Pat nor I has a sweet tooth, so Diana would eat the fruit, cereal, yogurt, biscuits, cheese, sliced meats, and French bread I always kept on hand. Some days she brought her own lunch.

One evening as I was heating up a pot of beef stew I'd prepared the day before, I discovered that all the chunks of meat were missing. Diana had picked them out for lunch. Clearly, back then she preferred meat to vegetables, just like my eighteen-year-old son, Patrick, today. It was eight o'clock by then and all the shops were closed. I was stuck for dinner that night. As I recall, we had what had become vegetable soup. The next time Diana came to work, I told her that it was no problem, but I'd discovered rather late that we couldn't have what I'd planned for dinner on Monday evening. She was more than welcome to anything in the house, but would she please let me know if she had finished any particular item so I could replace it before the stores closed. Evidently she did not do a lot of basic cooking herself. Ever polite and agreeable, she replied, "Yes, of course, Mrs. Robertson. So sorry to have inconvenienced you."

In keeping with her fresh and wholesome good looks, Diana wore simple, casual clothes to work, since she was playing with Patrick on the floor, feeding him in the kitchen, and pushing his stroller to the parks nearby. This meant Shetland sweaters and skirts or pants with a woolen coat in the winter and cotton prints in the summer, always with low-heeled loafers or flats. She used only a little, very discreet eye makeup; her skin looked wonderful on its own. She had fabulous thick dark blond hair with a great short haircut. She was terrifically pretty and always well groomed. Still, I would never have predicted the stunning, slim, polished beauty she became.

Diana's voice was marvelous—soft and low and a bit breathy with a beautiful upper-class accent. She used a few phrases that I particularly liked and still remember. When she needed a favor, such as leaving early, and I agreed, as I always did, she would say, "That's *very* kind of you, Mrs. Robertson." When she really disliked something, she would use the word "loathe," as in, "I simply loathe horses." Her favorite expression of approval or emotion was "tremendous" or "tremendously." If something was a real challenge, she would describe it as "daunting." When I gave her a suggestion or instructions, she would reply eagerly and politely, "Yes, of course, Mrs. Robertson." Her cultured voice and crisp, elegant accent made every sentence sound special. And I loved the way she always called me "Mrs. Robertson." She had such natural and flawless manners.

Within our comfortable relationship, Diana guarded her privacy carefully. For instance, she did not give me her address until we were moving back to New York at the end of the year. It turned out, of course, she lived in a much nicer building than we did. She had told me during her interview that she would not baby-sit in the evenings or on weekends. Clearly she valued her personal time. Once she deftly avoided telling me the name of her hairdresser when I complimented her on her haircut and asked where she had it done. She referred vaguely to a "little shop near my flat." I knew I couldn't push. She rarely mentioned her family and never mentioned her mother. If her younger brother, Charles, was in town from boarding school, she would ask to leave early to see him. She was devoted to him. She never mentioned he was at Eton, the best-known of the exclusive boarding schools in England.

One day she mentioned that she had taken Patrick to Kensington to play with her sister's baby daughter, but carefully omitted telling me that her sister lived in Kensington Palace and was married to the Queen's assistant private secretary. She simply said, "Today I took Patrick to play with my sister Jane's baby girl in Kensington." I was left to assume that Jane was an ordinary young mother living in a small town house, similar to those I had seen as rentals. When I took

Patrick to play at the duck pond in Kensington Gardens a few hundred yards from Kensington Palace, I would gaze at Christopher Wren's elegant, balanced architecture, never dreaming that my son had been visiting inside.

Diana always came to work bright-eyed, well rested, and on time. She'd told me she shared her flat with three other girls. While she did not offer many details about her social life, she said enough to give me a picture of a happy, relaxed young woman talking, giggling, and having fun with her roommates and other friends. It was clear that late hours, drinking, and serious boyfriends had no part in her life. She was a very wholesome, innocent young lady.

On Monday mornings in nice weather, Diana would ask, "Where did you go this weekend, Mrs. Robertson?" She knew we made frequent trips outside London. Other English friends would tell us about their favorite spots, but Diana was not forthcoming with travel suggestions. At the time, I assumed that she might not have seen as much of England and Scotland as we did during that year. Diana enjoyed our enthusiasm for her country—its natural beauty, its stately homes and castles, its history. She must have smiled inside when I would tell her of my pleasure in the architecture, paintings, and furniture I saw in England's famous mansions. She'd grown up in one! And she would always ask, "How did Patrick enjoy . . . Warwick Castle or Canterbury Cathedral or Dartmoor?" Patrick was a very good-natured sightseer.

In return, I would ask, "And how was your weekend?", leaving it up to her to say as little or as much as she chose. I would not have asked specifically, "What did you do last weekend?" She would answer politely and briefly, "Fine," or "Lovely," maybe mentioning that she'd been out in the country. Of course, I didn't know "the country" meant a huge estate that had been in the family for centuries. Diana was unfailingly polite but sparing of any details. She considered her personal life just that, personal. She was careful never to give us a clue about her background. If she did not volunteer information, something in her manner told me I should not intrude. She may not have even been aware of this perception I had. I viewed her understated manner as appealing and discreet, not as offputting or unfriendly.

Clearly, Diana did not want us to know who she was. We may possibly have been the only people Diana ever knew who had no idea *who* she was. We welcomed her into our home and trusted her with our child for *what* she was. This may have been one reason she stayed in touch with us over the years.

Along with Diana's discretion about her social life, I was aware of a natural delicacy or refinement that guarded her innermost feelings. I considered her emotional distance a sign of respect for her own privacy and that of others. She would not readily impose her problems on others. I thought this aura was her most intriguing quality. In retrospect, it is a great shame that she did not share the hurts and anguish of her early married life much sooner.

Diana's only shortcoming was that occasionally she would have one of her roommates, usually Carolyn Pride, call me on a Sunday evening to tell me that Diana would be unable to come to work the next day because she (Diana) was still out of town for the weekend. Fortunately, Nanny Chapman was happy to fill in on short notice, so these cancellations did not become a big problem. I'm sure Diana appreciated the flexibility that working for me provided. I knew she was young and needed time off, although a bit more advance warning would have been welcome. Really all that mattered to me was that she and Patrick adored each other. I felt no envy at their closeness. Rather, I loved to see the obvious delight they took in each other.

I must admit Patrick was a wonderful baby—happy, healthy, bright, and affectionate. When I took him out, other women would often stop and compliment me on my handsome, smiling child. And I would, of course, thank them but sometimes think, "What a shame Patrick doesn't have a younger mummy like Diana!" They made such an attractive pair. Sadly, I have just realized that during the year Diana worked for us, I was the same age, thirty-six, that she was when she died. What a sobering thought.

Various relatives came to visit us in London that year. My husband's parents came from Houston in April and were simply enchanted by Diana. My mother-in-law, Betty, is friendly, talkative, and direct. As she chatted with Diana, Betty learned that Diana was eighteen and unattached and announced to her that she had a tall, eligible son in college back in Texas. Mike was six feet four inches to Diana's five feet ten inches. Recalling this conversation later, Betty and I couldn't decide whether to laugh or blush about the fact that she had tried to arrange a blind date for the young woman who soon after became engaged to the heir to the British throne.

Betty has recalled for me other conversations she had with Diana that spring that further show how genuine and unassuming Diana was. After shopping at Harrod's one day Betty returned to our flat with a half dozen Shetland sweaters she thought she'd found at a great price—only forty-eight dollars each! Diana very sweetly pointed out that there was an English pound sign on the label, not a dollar sign. The "bargain" sweaters had cost more than one hundred dollars each, more than the price back in Houston. When Betty inquired about buying a kilt in the Robertson plaid at the Scotch House near Harrod's, Diana explained that an authentic kilt wrapped from the left to the right. Diana also recommended a hairdresser for my mother-in-law, though not the one she herself used. According to Betty, Diana was "dying to visit America." Betty, of course, urged, "You have to see Houston and when you do, you must stay with us, so you won't have a big hotel bill."

I'm sure Diana never forgot her exposure to honest-to-goodness Texans. And Diana never did see Texas.

During my in-laws' visit, Patrick would cry when Diana left for the day, leaving him to stay with his loving grandparents until I came home from work—a clear sign of how devoted he was to his young nanny. Betty and Pat were dismayed, at first. Patrick was their first grandchild and they adored him, while he apparently preferred Diana's company to theirs. Once they grew to know her, they found the situation touching and amusing.

My brother, Peter, stayed with us for two full weeks and left so early each day to explore London that he never once laid eyes on her. And my own husband saw her only twice in passing at the end of the day. Needless to say, they both regret not getting to know her better that year.

C H A P T E R

3

*W*e discovered quite by accident that Diana was blue-blooded and titled . One evening in June, as I was straightening up the living room, I found a bank deposit slip tucked under the skirt of the sofa. The slip bore the name "Coutts and Company," whom I'd learned at work were bankers to the Queen and the aristocracy. Imprinted on the front was "Lady Diana Spencer." I looked again and thought, "Hmm, I'd better look into this title." I assumed the slip had fallen out of her handbag by accident.

I said nothing the next day, but I took the deposit slip along to my bank to see if my fellow officers could shed any light on the situation. We went to look up Diana in *Burke's Peerage*, a reference book on the English nobility. We discovered that Diana was one of three daughters of the Earl

Spencer and belonged to one of the oldest and most illustrious families in England. I already knew that after the royal family, dukes had the highest rank; just below them were earls, and there were very few of either rank. I simply couldn't believe that a young woman of such an aristocratic background was probably giving lunch to my son at that very moment. The English bankers with whom I worked were equally floored.

Then I faced a true dilemma. Should I ignore this information or should I mention the deposit slip to her? It was particularly tricky since I had no way of knowing how the darn thing had appeared underneath the sofa in the first place or if she had noticed it missing. It was one of those, "I know. She knows. But does she know that I know?" situations.

I felt slightly intimidated by her social position, even though we did not belong to the English class structure. I mean, what *do* you do when you discover someone you employ has the sort of lineage and social position you've only read about? More importantly, I did not want our relationship to change in any way. As friendly and trusting as that relationship was, I was still the parent setting the guidelines.

After another few days, I was so uncomfortable with the ambiguity of the situation that I returned the deposit slip, mentioning that I'd found it tangled up in the sofa. There was no discussion of how it had landed there. Then I said,

"It's quite a surprise for us to have you with your impressive background, I mean a title and all, looking after Patrick." She smiled, gestured with a toss of her right hand, and said, "Oh, that." The subject never came up again. It meant nothing to her.

She was unpretentious and natural at eighteen and continued to be so, always. In 1980, Diana was a happy, normal teenager, enjoying her first experience of independence, busy with her two child-care jobs, and having fun with her friends. My new knowledge made no difference at all in our relationship.

At the end of June, we had to move from our flat. Exxon had extended my husband's assignment for another six months and the landlord wanted a huge rent increase that the company would not cover. At the beginning of July, we moved to 11 Eaton Mews South, a small carriage house I had found. The house was owned by an American expatriate, Jud James, who had installed new appliances and cleaned all the curtains and carpets for us—a considerable improvement over the flat. Jud was proud of the fact that earlier on he had leased his house for a while to Richard Leakey, the famous anthropologist. I wonder how Jud felt when the young nanny in his house became engaged to the Prince of Wales.

The mews house was sunnier and more attractively furnished than the flat had been. As she walked up the spiral stairs on her first day there, Diana commented, "What an improvement this place is!" We laughed together about the huge difference between the gloomy, uncomfortable flat my husband had chosen and the cheerful, cozy house I had found. The house was only a few blocks from our first flat, so Diana could still take Patrick to the private "key" garden in Belgrave Square, a definite plus during the summer months.

Toward the end of July, Diana agreed to baby-sit for Patrick into the early evening as a favor to me. The next day she was traveling to Scotland for her summer holiday, leaving me in a bit of a bind for daytime child care. That particular evening, I desperately needed a sitter. A good friend from The Morgan Bank, Lee Thistlethwaite, had invited me to see *The Magic Flute* at the Glyndebourne Opera House, south of London near the coast. Lee's girlfriend at the time, who later became his wife, had already seen the opera twice with him. He was scheduled to entertain banking clients that evening and thought I might enjoy a night out. The problem was that my husband was in New York on business and Nanny Chapman could not come until later that evening. Since Lee and I had to leave London before five o'clock to miss rush-hour traffic, Diana agreed to stay with Patrick until Nanny Chapman appeared.

When Lee arrived to pick me up, I introduced Diana simply as Diana Spencer. They exchanged a few brief words while I kissed Patrick good-bye, and off we went. As we struggled through the southbound traffic in Lewes, Lee and I had a conversation about Diana that seems both remarkable and humorous in retrospect.

I started out by saying, "Lee, you'll never believe who my nanny is." Then I told him about Diana's title and background and how amazed and grateful I was that she was looking after Patrick so sweetly and carefully. Lee and I agreed that she was awfully pretty and down to earth.

I mentioned that she did not appear to have a steady boyfriend, and perhaps Lee might want to give her a call. Lee had a very respectable background—a good public school, university, solid career prospects, and a father who'd retired from the foreign service. Lee chuckled at my naïveté and explained that in England the social gulf between the daughter of an earl and a commoner was so great that he would never presume to ask Diana out. He reiterated that her social position and lineage were as exalted as they could possibly be. "In fact," he added, "with her background, she'd be a suitable match for Prince Andrew."

Direct as usual, I replied, "Forget about Prince Andrew. If her background's as impeccable as you say, she ought to be a match for Prince Charles. She'd be *perfect* as the next queen of England!" Then touching on a critical qualification for any future queen, I added, "And I'd bet my life on her virtue."

That August, Diana sent us two postcards from Scotland. She did not tell us she was spending part of her holiday at Balmoral with her sister, Lady Jane Fellowes, and her family in close proximity to the royal family. The first postcard was a portrait of the third Earl Spencer by Sir Joshua Reynolds from the collection at Althorp, Diana's family home. Diana chose the picture as a small joke. She knew we had visited numerous stately homes and castles around England. When I had asked her if we should include Althorp in our travels, she had said, "I shouldn't bother." I read years later that the Spencer children were very unhappy about their stepmother's redecorating at Althorp and the decision to open their family home to the public. So, the postcard was as close as we ever got to Althorp. Her second card wished us a good holiday—we were going to Devon—and told us she was "missing Patrick."

4

*W*hen Diana returned to work on Monday, September 16, she came directly up to my bedroom and announced, "Mrs. Robertson, I have something important to tell you." I could see out of the corner of my eye that she had a slight, mischievous grin on her face.

"Go right ahead," I said as I continued to blow-dry my hair in front of the mirror above the dresser.

"No, Mrs. Robertson, I'd like your full attention." I switched off my hair dryer and faced her as she stood in the doorway. "When you leave for work this morning, you'll notice a lot of reporters and photographers at the entrance to the mews."

I wondered aloud if the press were following either Lord Vestey, a notorious international financier, or John

Browne, a bright young M.P. known as one of "Maggie's boys," both of whom lived on our small street.

"No, actually, Mrs. Robertson, they're waiting for me," Diana said with a great deal of blushing, staring at the floor, and throat clearing.

"Good heavens, Diana, why?"

"Well . . . I spent last weekend at Balmoral."

"With Prince Andrew?" I asked, remembering my friend Lee's comment on the way to Glyndebourne.

"No, actually, I was there to see Prince Charles." More blushes and throat clearing, quickly followed by her disclaimer, "But *he* didn't invite me. His *mother* did." Hearing Diana speak of Her Majesty the Queen as "his mother" certainly gave me a clear picture of the circles in which Diana moved.

I gasped and asked, probably rather tactlessly, "Gosh, do you think there's any chance of a romance developing?"

"Not really," she said with noticeable regret. "After all, he's thirty-one and I'm only nineteen. He'd never look seriously at me." So modest, so appealing. I couldn't imagine him not learning to love her. We certainly had.

"Well, Diana, I wouldn't be so sure," I replied, thinking of my prediction from July.

As I left for my office a few minutes later, I saw a dozen or so photographers and reporters clustered outside the white stucco arch that marked the entrance to the mews. They had followed Diana from her flat when she came to work. On that first morning, the press were a small, polite group waiting hopefully for Diana to reappear later in the day. She and I both thought this initial flurry of interest would soon fade. I barely noticed them as I caught a taxi to work.

Now, it is so poignant to think of Diana leaving my home with Patrick that day and braving the press for the very first time, determined to carry on her life as usual.

From that day on, Diana's life became more complicated and stressful, and so did mine. As Diana continued to be linked with Prince Charles, the press moved to its regular stakeout at her apartment building. They generally did not follow her to my house after that first day. Still, I worried that Diana might be distracted if the reporters followed her. I asked her to be extra careful with Patrick, especially crossing streets. Some mornings she would call to say she would not be coming to work because she simply could not face the growing number of reporters and photographers waiting outside her flat. Then I would call my office to tell them that I would not be coming to work that day. My fellow workers at the Saudi International Bank didn't mind my absences because they thought it was quite exciting that my nanny was linked with Prince Charles.

As the pressures on her built up, she shared some of her concerns with me, asking for my advice. I'd learned to give her my immediate and full attention when she wanted to talk.

First of all, she was terribly worried about making a misstep with the press. She knew she had to be pleasant and polite at all times but could not afford to say a word. "My sister, Sarah, spoke to the press and frankly, Mrs. Robertson, that was the end of her." Diana's older sister, Lady Sarah, had been involved with Prince Charles in 1978. She had given a magazine interview declaring that she was not in love with him and would turn him down if he proposed. Whether these were her true feelings or she was playing hard to get was not important. Her unguarded speech was considered indiscreet by the palace, and her relationship with Prince Charles was finished. Lady Sarah was very inquisitive about Diana's romance with Prince Charles. As a result, Diana confided one day, "I don't even dare to pick up the telephone at my flat for fear it might be Sarah." I inferred that Diana was uncomfortable with her sister's curiosity because Lady Sarah was jealous of her little sister at that time.

Another morning Diana and I sat together on the window seat in our second-floor living room, looking out at a chilly, gray November day. She cleared her throat gently and asked, "Mrs. Robertson, I wonder if I might ask your advice on something, since you're so much . . . er, older and . . . wiser, I mean." She said that her grandmother had suggested to Diana that she seek help from Buckingham Palace in dealing with the press. Diana did not tell me that her grandmother was Lady Ruth Fermoy, a lady-in-waiting to the Queen Mother. Diana wanted to use our telephone to discuss this further with her grandmother. In the meantime, "Do *you* think I should ask Charles for help, Mrs. Robertson?" She was quite calm and in control; she simply wanted another opinion.

I thought for a minute, then told her, "I wouldn't ask for help if I could possibly manage without it. You're handling yourself so beautifully on your own. If the palace thinks you can't handle the pressure now, they might think you couldn't handle it once you're part of the royal family. If you're serious about this romance, you should try to struggle along on your own." That conversation took place in early November on the day that the photograph of Diana pushing Patrick up the mews in his stroller was taken. It is my favorite photograph of the two of them because it reminds me of the trust she demonstrated that day.

I clearly recall thinking at that point, "This child needs a mother for guidance." I had learned from the newspapers that her own mother lived up in Scotland with her second husband. She had not been an integral part of Diana's life for some years. I hoped that Diana was receiving sensible advice from other people, perhaps her sister, Lady Jane Fellowes. By then I knew from the newspapers that Lady Jane was married to the Queen's assistant private secretary. She had to know about matters pertaining to the royal family. At that time in her life, Diana was closer to Lady Jane than to Lady Sarah. This changed in the last few years of

Diana's life, as I was to learn when I was in London for her funeral.

As for her views on Prince Charles, Diana thought he was absolutely "wonderful," almost "perfect," but that he had to "work too hard." She wished that she could see him more often. Since she and Charles had few meetings that fall, and almost none of them were private, her infatuation with him must have been based on her romantic image of him combined with his lofty position. He was, after all, the "most eligible bachelor in the world." Who wouldn't be impressed? I must say that Prince Charles has great personal charm and presence. I have met him on three occasions and found him to be gracious, unaffected, and witty. He seems quite genuine, although that impression may come from his being well schooled in putting people at ease. No matter. He does it flawlessly and convincingly.

One morning Diana came to work with a Barbara Cartland romance novel tucked under her arm. Coincidentally, Ms. Cartland was the mother of the Earl of Spencer's second wife, Raine, whom I was to learn years later in the press the Spencer children had detested at first. I hoped that novel did not represent Diana's only reading interests. I knew from the newspapers that Prince Charles had also been seeing Amanda Knatchbull, the niece of Charles's much admired and recently deceased great-uncle, Lord Mountbatten. The papers implied that Amanda was better educated and more sophisticated than Diana and represented a real threat to Diana's chances with Charles. Tactfully, I suggested to her that she upgrade her reading choices and perhaps "scan the *Times* or the *Daily Telegraph* each day to learn a bit about current events, if you want to keep up with Prince Charles."

I knew from the press that Prince Charles was cultivated and well educated. He had attended Cambridge University, one of the world's most prestigious universities. It was well-known that he had many cultural and intellectual pursuits—opera, architecture, philosophy, gardening, and painting. He was an accomplished diplomat and world traveler. He loved horses and spent a great deal of time playing polo and hunting.

Diana at nineteen was really too young and too sketchily educated to have developed her own serious interests. I never doubted that she would find her own causes as she matured. From what I had observed, it seemed clear that her focus would be people—issues concerning children, health, and possibly education. She would lead from her heart, not from her head, as she said of herself years later. I could see this in her all those years ago. I hoped that if Diana and Prince Charles married, they would find interests in common besides their royal duties and their children.

One day that fall, she brought along a swatch of a beautiful silk pink-striped fabric and asked, "Do you think this is pretty?" I certainly did. She seemed pleased by my approval and said, "Good. I'm wearing this to a party tonight." She gave no further details. The newspapers the next day mentioned Diana's appearance at Princess Margaret's fiftieth birthday party at the Ritz. They felt it was significant that the Lady Diana had been included in this private royal celebration. I saw in a picture book much later that she had worn a dress made from that pink fabric to the birthday party at the Ritz. What I especially liked was that over her gossamer pink ball gown she had worn a simple green loden cloth coat, showing that she was still very much the schoolgirl despite her aristocratic socializing. The only time she had specifically told me about her social plans was in July. She had asked for a day off to attend a garden party at Buckingham Palace at which she would formally meet Her Majesty, the Queen.

Diana had one dislike that would soon set her at odds with the royal family. She loved animals, except for horses. As I mentioned earlier, she told me, "I simply loathe horses." She had had a bad fall from a horse at a young age and had disliked the animals ever since. She also loathed the traditional English country pastimes of hunting and shooting. She was simply too tenderhearted to hurt any living thing. I loved this about her, as I feel the same way.

Diana and I talked, naturally, about children and parenting. Her personal dream at this early time in her life was to have "a dozen children." I admired her energy and commitment. I was worn out by one child, but then I was much older than she, thirty-seven to her nineteen.

One issue I had to face that fall was whether or not to return to full-time work once we moved back to New York in December. My husband and I very much wished to remain in London—we loved living there. All year expatriate friends had told us stories about families who had come to London for a short assignment and were still living there ten or twelve years later. We hoped we'd fall into that group. No such luck. Exxon wanted Pat back in New York.

I had not been happy working full-time for those few months in 1979 and feeling that Patrick was a stranger when I came home after a twelve-hour day. Working only two days a week had given me so much more time with my son. It was such a joy to be with him. I did not want to give up that closeness ever again. I discussed this life-defining decision endlessly with my husband, of course, and with Diana as well. Fortunately, my husband and I had a very modest lifestyle for a two-income couple. We decided we would forgo a bigger house, better cars, and vacations so that I could stay home with Patrick.

I knew deep down I could not bear to see my son being raised full-time by anyone else. I'd tried it and even under the best of circumstances—caring, reliable help and little travel—I didn't want it. I'd been lucky to find Chris the previous year, but she was now working for a friend and I couldn't get her back. Maybe if I could have brought Diana or Nanny Chapman back with me, I would have felt differently. Maybe being older and having already achieved a reasonable degree of success in a career made a difference. Still, it was a difficult decision for me and one I've reexamined from time to time ever since. I've missed the wonderful people with whom I have worked and the intellectual challenge of corporate life. I quickly sent a resignation letter to The Morgan Bank in October before I could return to work and be tempted to stay. I showed my letter to Diana, who concurred heartily with my decision, but showed surprising empathy with how difficult my choice had been, saying, "I know how much your career means to you."

One peripheral aspect of the royal romance was the reaction of the two neighbors in the mews with whom I had an acquaintance. Patrick was the only child on the street and was a good excuse for a doorstep visit. One woman was an older American expatriate living permanently in London. She agreed that Diana was lovely and eminently suitable, but that Prince Charles was likely to marry a European princess if a non-Catholic could be found. She thought Diana's chances were slim. I disagreed, of course.

The other neighbor was the beautiful, charming, and well-bred wife, now ex-wife, of the M.P. John Browne. Elizabeth was familiar with the circles in which Diana moved and with her family background. One gloomy afternoon in November she invited me for a traditional English tea with bone china, a silver tea service, and dainty sandwiches. She filled me in on the bits of Diana's family history that I might not have gathered from the London newspa-

pers, including her parents' bitter divorce, the Earl's remar-
riage, and Lady Sarah's earlier romance with Prince
Charles. I must stress that this was done in a very kind and
supportive way, not gossipy or mean. Much of what she
told me had been in the London newspapers that fall.
Elizabeth liked what she knew of Diana and sympathized
with the pressures on her. She simply thought I might want
or need to know a bit more about my child's nanny.

While Diana remained poised and calm in front of the
press, in private she cared desperately about Prince Charles
and the outcome of the courtship. She expressed her concern to me: "I will simply die if this doesn't work out. I
won't be able to show my face." This statement implied that
she was uncertain of his affection that fall. She never mentioned any concern about other women he might have been
seeing at the time. She was, as I've said, a very private and
discreet person. If she wanted to talk, she would. I would
never have pried.

Diana was the new face in Prince Charles's social life
that year, so the hopes of the public and the press were
high. She was clearly in love and definitely committed to
the relationship. I imagined that she, like any young woman
in love, would have welcomed a commitment from him as
soon as possible. It may have been presumptuous of me,
but impulsively I promised her that she could stay with us
in America "if this doesn't work out and we will hide you
away until it all blows over." I knew she'd enjoyed skiing

during her time in Switzerland, so I suggested a ski holiday in the Rocky Mountains as a diversion. I don't imagine it was much consolation to her, knowing the huge stakes involved in the courtship.

Naively, I believed that Prince Charles and Diana had a very good chance at happiness. They had each experienced a lonely, often unhappy childhood. Hers was scarred at a young age by her parents' bitter divorce. She had missed the hugs and cuddles she so gladly gave to my child. Charles had also missed out on parental warmth and support, with a distant mother and a domineering father. I believed that they would give each other the tenderness, warmth, and security each had missed growing up. I was sure that raising a family would bind them together, as it had for me and my husband. I knew Diana would certainly bring love, caring, and commitment to her marriage along with her love of children. Now, it is clear that Diana married for love. Sadly, Prince Charles did not. I still find it hard to believe that they were unable to find a common ground for friendship, parenting, and an amicable working relationship. Perhaps without the presence of a third party and the media exposure, they might have succeeded.

As December 1980 and our departure loomed, Diana kept to her baby-sitting schedule and more. I caught a serious viral infection and could not even sit up in bed for a week. Not only did I miss any going-away parties and an evening at the House of Commons with our M.P. neighbor, but I was too weak to pack up our personal belongings for air shipment. Diana pitched in cheerfully and packed up Patrick's toys, books, and clothes.

Typically thoughtful, Diana brought us a going-away present, a dark green leather-bound photograph album with "1980" stamped in gold because, as she said, "I know you've taken lots of photos as you've traveled around England this year." The most poignant photos were, of course, the two I had snapped of Diana holding Patrick in our living room in October. I wanted to remember her as our nanny, regardless of her future position. I certainly wish I'd taken dozens more, but I did not want to seem intrusive. The pictures I did take clearly show her natural beauty and her tender attitude toward Patrick.

Diana came over to see us off the morning we left for the airport. The four of us stood in our lower hallway saying good-bye with lots of hugs and good wishes. Diana and I were both in tears, as she held Patrick close and said she would miss him "tremendously." We promised to write to each other and keep up our friendship.

Not until later would Diana realize that the past year of being on her own in London and caring for Patrick would be, as she was to say, "the happiest year of my life." I hugged her and assured her, "We'll think of you every day and pray for good news from London soon. But," I continued, "we care very much for you and will help you in any way we can, whatever happens."

When Diana and I parted that gray December morning, we did not know what the future would bring or that this would not be our last meeting. She was very young and unspoiled. I thought she was on the brink of a fairy-tale life of splendor and joy.

Neither of us could have imagined then the despair that her new life would bring.

*B*y Christmas, our family of three was resettled in our little house in Bronxville.

The year in London had passed quickly. We had a quiet Christmas and became reacquainted with our neighbors. It was very comforting to be home again, surrounded by familiar furniture, pictures, and books. Patrick, now walking and climbing everywhere, was happy to have more play space indoors and his own large yard outdoors. We discovered that a family of raccoons had taken over that yard in our absence. It was several days before we dared to venture into our own garden.

Patrick and I were invited to join a playgroup with three other toddlers, all boys. With these three mothers as well as a few from our neighborhood, I was happy to have a wider circle of women friends than I had had in London. I was adjusting slowly to the loss of professional companionship I had enjoyed while working in New York and London. Our peaceful suburban community, no matter how pretty and green and safe, was no match for cosmopolitan London. I missed our long walks through historic neighborhoods and parks, the vibrant pace of a world-class city, the easy access to museums and cathedrals for a cultural lift, and our wonderful excursions to every corner of England and Scotland. However, I had chosen to devote myself to raising Patrick, so I cheerfully prepared to settle into my life as a stay-at-home mother.

Once again, my situation changed with a phone call. This time the call was from David Jeffrey, who had been my first boss at The Morgan Bank in 1975 and had become a good friend. David had left the bank to start his own financial consulting firm the same month I had started my maternity leave, in May of 1979. His business was booming and he needed help meeting customer needs, primarily financial reports and credit training for smaller U.S. and foreign banks. Part-time work in London had been a good balance for me, so I was happy to help David. I continued to do so off and on for the next ten years.

Once more, I needed a part-time caretaker, but no Diana appeared this time. I did find a mature, friendly, experienced sitter from the neighboring town, who came for her interview and called me "Mary" right from the start. "It's so funny that

Diana always called you 'Mrs. Robertson,'" my husband humorously observed, "And the new sitter and all the repairmen and shopkeepers call you 'Mary.'" We missed Diana dreadfully! We missed her tenderness and special feeling for Patrick, her gentle disposition, her lovely presence in our home. Having Diana as such an essential part of our life in London had certainly helped to make 1980 one of the best years of my life.

In mid-January, we were surprised and touched when we received a letter on blue airmail paper from Diana at her flat at 60 Coleherne Court. She wrote, "I can never thank you enough, Mrs. Robertson, for being so kind and understanding with the whole of Fleet Street following me!! . . . Never have I adored looking after a child (more) than Patrick and thank you for providing such happiness over the year for me!" We couldn't believe she was thinking of us at such a stressful time in her life. We knew from the press that the royal courtship was still on, but there was no word of an engagement yet. Diana must have been feeling such pressure not only from the uncertainty of the courtship but also from the continuing media speculation about her chances of succeeding where so many had failed. She did not say a word about any of this in her letter. We were touched that she missed us as much as we missed her. We kept our fingers crossed and eagerly scanned the newspapers and magazines for news of an engagement between Diana and Charles.

Then, late in the morning of February 24, I answered the telephone in my bedroom and heard the voice of a friend in London . . . "Mary, it's Dena. Your girl made it!" I knew she meant that Diana's engagement to Prince Charles had just been announced. I gave a big shout and literally jumped for joy, banging my head on the low dormer ceiling. I couldn't have been prouder of Diana if I'd been her mother. I was so happy for her I could have burst! I knew how desperately she had wished for this outcome. The past fall, she had told me that she would "simply die" if the romance didn't work out. How wonderful that her dream had come true.

Almost immediately, a mischievous picture popped into my mind of the future and royal Diana, scheduled for an official day of handshaking, ribbon cutting, or tree planting and wishing she could have a friend call to cancel those tedious engagements. As Princess of Wales, she would not be able to cancel on short notice, if at all, as she had when she was baby-sitting for me. I wondered how the lively, spontaneous, and very young Diana would adjust to her official duties. I felt a bit sorry for her as I dimly realized how rigid and structured her new life might be.

Pat and I, of course, could barely grasp that the Diana who'd been Patrick's beloved nanny three short months ago was destined to be the next queen of England. What a leap! From the nursery to the palace. Positively daunting.

I wrote immediately to give her our best wishes. At the

time Pat and I assumed, as Diana clearly did, that she would fulfill her role in the traditional way. She would be a dutiful and supportive wife, deferring to her husband most of the time, and a devoted mother to the many children she wished for. There was nothing in my experience of her to indicate how *very* different her path would be.

Somewhat selfishly, I admit, I was sorry to contemplate losing contact with Diana. When she and I had parted in December, we'd promised to stay in touch. It never occurred to me that now, in her new life as a royal princess, we would ever hear from or see her again. She had moved into too rarefied an orbit to include our family.

Pat and I felt confident that she would be an enormous success. Diana certainly had the family breeding and lovely presence to join the royal family. With her fresh, unspoiled beauty and grace, she would look and act every inch the fairy-tale princess.

The young Diana was not yet well informed about national issues or world affairs, but she would absorb this knowledge as she gained experience. Her background and poise would ensure that she would always say and do the right thing, even if she was quaking inside. She would certainly charm guests in receiving lines at state ceremonies or dinner partners at formal banquets. And we naturally assumed she would receive training and advice from the royal family and palace staff. All in all, we believed she was destined for a traditional royal life of luxury, duty, and security—just what she had dreamed of the previous fall.

In those very early days, the world was already demanding "star" quality of a young and unprepared Diana. Over time, the surprise would be how brilliantly she exceeded those early expectations.

For our part, we thought we would be following her path from a distance in the press. Our friends called to tell us when the photo of Diana pushing Patrick in his stroller appeared in *Newsweek*, or when our name was mentioned in a news magazine or paper. We were generally mislabeled as the Robinsons. Everyone asked if we would be going to the wedding, and we would reply, "Us? No, of course not." We truly never expected to hear from Diana again, so her January letter became especially precious to us.

We were stunned when a letter from Diana on Buckingham Palace stationery arrived in late March. She was clearly happy, writing, "I am on a cloud." She missed Patrick "dreadfully." She hoped that we were all "settled down by now, including your cat too—." Diana had never even *seen* our cat. We'd left him with my brother because England requires a six-month quarantine for cats and dogs. How did she *ever* remember we had one?

Then, "I will be sending you an invitation to the wedding, naturally. . . ." The *wedding . . . naturally . . .* God bless her. Maybe we weren't going to lose her after all. She even asked me to send a picture of Patrick to show to "her intended(!), since I'm always talking about him." As for her engagement, she could never even have imagined it the year before. She closed with her typical and appealing modesty: "I do hope you don't mind me writing to you but just had to let you know what was going on."

Mind? I was thrilled and touched and amazed by her fondness and thoughtfulness, as I have been every single time she has written to us and seen us. This was always to be the Diana we knew and loved—kind, affectionate, unpretentious.

I wrote back right away and sent her the two photographs I'd taken of her holding Patrick in our living room the previous fall. After Diana received the photographs, she wrote back on March 31 to thank me and sent us their official engagement picture. She said I should throw the photograph away if it was of no use. She added, "You said some lovely things which I don't feel I deserve. . . ." Surely, she knew from the previous year that we would be her devoted friends forever.

An incident that spring involving our other London baby-sitter, Beth Chapman, illustrated how tenderhearted and thoughtful Diana always was. Nanny Chapman had been losing weight drastically that past fall, and we learned early in 1981 from her daughter, Penny Portlock of Norwich, that Nanny Chapman had terminal cancer. Penny wrote us that her mother was so proud to have "shared a baby" with the future Princess of Wales. Diana and Mrs. Chapman had met a few times when baby-sitting shifts switched over late in the day. I mentioned this sad situation in a letter to Diana, who promptly wrote to Nanny Chapman at her nursing home and sent a personalized photograph as well. Soon after, Penny informed us, sadly, of her mother's death and told us that Diana's letter and photograph had made her mother the envy of her hospital ward and had greatly brightened her mother's final weeks. I then wrote to Diana to thank her for her kindness.

As the spring progressed, Pat and I eagerly waited for our invitation to the wedding. We were afraid something might go wrong. In late May, we received another sweet letter from Diana, exclaiming, "How terribly exciting that Patrick is now beginning to speak, only wish I could witness it. . . ." In the same letter she observed, "Every fitting of my wedding dress has to be taken in—I'm sure it has alot to do with nervous energy and there is *plenty* of that!" She was hoping for an end to the public pressures after the wedding and couldn't wait to get away from other people on their honeymoon. Diana had no idea that the engagement was only the beginning of a life that would be relentlessly in the public eye. She naively believed that once the excitement of the wedding died down and she was sheltered within the royal family, the press would lose interest.

I could relate to her prewedding jitters and stress. Losing *some* weight would have been all right. She was clearly going to be in front of a lens a great deal of the time, and the camera does add ten pounds. My Diana-watching friends had commented on the youthful "puppy fat" that had shown clearly in the now infamous black strapless gown she had worn to her first public engagement. This was a charity gala for the Royal Opera House at London's Goldsmiths' Hall on the night she first met Princess Grace of Monaco, a woman she grew to admire greatly. I viewed the weight loss she had mentioned later in her letter as temporary and understandable. She probably did too, at that time. I had no idea of the stress and loneliness she was already enduring behind the palace walls.

Diana also mentioned how much she had missed Prince Charles while he'd been away on an official trip for several weeks. She was glad to have him back near her, "where he belongs." In those early days, Diana assumed her husband would be at her side to care for and guide her. In a television interview during her engagement, she had said, "With Prince Charles by my side, I know I cannot go wrong." She needed and expected his support. If only her expectations had been met.

Finally, in late May or early June our breathlessly anticipated gilt-edged invitation to the July 29 wedding arrived. Soon after, we received a silver-edged card inviting us to a private formal ball at Buckingham Palace two nights before the wedding. We had been expecting the first invitation but were totally surprised by the second one. For both invitations, we had to reply to the Lord Chamberlain, Saint James's Palace, London, SW1. For the wedding, dress was specified as: Uniform, Morning Dress or Lounge Suit. For the ball, dress was: Uniform or Evening Dress. Tiaras Optional. We had no idea what a "lounge suit" was, nor did I have a tiara handy—fortunately tiaras were optional. Help! We needed advice about protocol and dress for these royal celebrations.

I racked my brain and remembered my most sophisticated and elegant friend from The Morgan Bank, Betsy Weinberg, later Smith. Betsy, a second Morgan banker, and I had shared a taxi pool from the East Fifties to Wall Street during my pre-Patrick, presuburban career days. Betsy was happy to help and called her grandmother. By a lucky circumstance, Betsy's grandfather had actually been the American ambassador to the Court of Saint James, the proper description for the position of ambassadors to Great Britain. We couldn't have found a more knowledgeable source.

Pat and I learned that the Queen is initially addressed as "Your Majesty" and any prince or princess as "Your Royal Highness," then as "Ma'am" or "Sir" if the conversation continues. Importantly, a person cannot approach or speak to a member of the royal family without a formal introduction. Bowing and curtsying to royalty is desirable, but not required, for Americans; this is not *our* monarchy, after all. Diana was still simply "Lady Diana" until her marriage. Betsy's grandmother suggested I wear long white leather gloves if I could find them—I couldn't. A lounge suit is simply a business suit. "Tiaras Optional" meant just that. The

aristocratic guests attending the gala would have tiaras of diamonds and other precious gems that had been in their families
for generations. The rest of us would be bareheaded. Anyone
can wear a tiara, but few people nowadays would need or
could afford one.

Pat already had a handsome tuxedo for the party and
for the wedding decided to rent morning dress, including a
gray top hat and suede gloves, from the well-known firm of
Moss Bros. in London. I, of course, had "nothing to wear."
I needed a new evening gown and gloves for the ball and a
new day dress and hat for the wedding. As Pat and I made
travel plans, we simply couldn't believe Diana had remembered us and invited us to what was already being called
"the wedding of the century."

One last dilemma was the choice of a wedding present.
What could we possibly send the royal couple that they
didn't already have? We decided something simple and
classic from Tiffany—a world-recognized name—would
work. We selected a sterling silver picture frame engraved
with the date of the wedding. So the frame wouldn't look
too bare, I placed a photograph of Patrick inside. I enclosed
a brief note wishing Diana happiness and suggesting she
might want to replace Patrick's picture with a photograph
of her own child when the time came. I didn't want her to
think that I felt we were so special that she would keep
Patrick's photograph forever.

We asked my mother to look after Patrick at our home

while we were away. We could not bring him with us because we had no one to look after him in London. Diana was otherwise occupied and Nanny Chapman had passed away. Our friends teased us about not being able to get a baby-sitter in London anymore.

We arranged to stay with Exxon friends, Dennis and Ceil Puglisi, in their Brompton Square flat. Ceil had been my constant companion on my nonworking days the year before, since we both had toddlers the same age. Close friends of Pat's parents, Jack and Laura Lee Blanton from Houston, in a typically thoughtful gesture, arranged for a driver and limousine to transport us to the ball and the wedding so we could arrive in style. We were all set.

The only small cloud on our horizon was that the press had discovered us in mid-July and besieged us the week before we left with phone calls. Reporters and photographers came to our front door and peered in our windows. These invasions of our privacy gave us a small taste of the pressure Diana had been under during the months before her engagement. I recall one particularly persistent woman reporter who verified that Diana had really been our nanny and then asked, "Are you telling me that those royal hands actually changed dirty diapers?" I didn't even answer her. We quickly formulated our statement: "We consider our relationship with Lady Diana to be a private matter and do not wish to discuss it." At Exxon, Jim Morakis from public affairs kindly gave us advice about security measures at home and arranged to have Pat's phone calles screened.

Then, to our horror, my mother-in-law, in a burst of pride and excitement, gave a lengthy interview to the *Houston Chronicle,* which was picked up by the wire services. We were worried Diana might find out and think *we* were talking to the press and calling attention to ourselves. I wrote to her immediately explaining the situation. I was anxious that she know we would *never* take advantage of her friendship. I didn't know if we'd actually see her at the ball to explain. Considering what Diana eventually became used to in the way of press exposure, this tiny faux pas would seem insignificant.

With a big hug for Patrick and my mother and a promise from the local police to keep an eye on our house to prevent press harassment, Pat and I flew to London on July 24 for what might well be the most glamorous few days of our lives.

∞

*W*hen we arrived in England, we could almost feel the excitement in the air. Banners, pictures, and other decorations hung everywhere, and the streets were packed with people waiting to celebrate the wedding of the century. The formal party in honor of the royal match was held on the evening of Monday, July 27—two nights before the wedding. That day I felt nervous with anticipation as I lunched with a friend and went to the hairdresser. Pat met Exxon colleagues for lunch near their office in Mayfair. As he described our plans for the upcoming ball and wedding, Pat began to feel totally overwhelmed by the importance and glamour of these royal events. So my darling husband excused himself, walked over to Green Park just across from the palace, and simply collapsed with nervous strain to nap on a quiet patch of grass for the afternoon. I've always envied his ability to tune out and relax when he's under stress; I get tense and can't eat or sleep.

That night we had an early supper with Dennis, our host, then dressed for the evening. I thought Pat looked very handsome in the Paul Stuart tuxedo I'd given him as a birthday present the year before. My evening gown was a sleeveless lavender taffeta with small ruffles around the arms and the hemline and a big bow at the waist. I've saved that dress all these years, and my daughter hopes to wear it one day. As I put on my little pearl earrings and a faux pearl necklace, I thought wistfully about the heirloom jewels I was likely to see later that evening.

I was glad I'd found long white fabric gloves to cover my poison ivy rash. Our normally indoor cat had recently escaped into a neighbor's yard. When I finally retrieved him, I got poison ivy all over my arms from his long, fluffy fur. What timing! Just when I needed to look my best, I'd contracted this itchy red rash. Pat teased me about my typical bad luck. Something unsightly always occurs on the few occasions when we have to look elegant. Once I gave myself a black eye by walking into a doorway. At least the rash was not on my face, and I could hide it under my gloves.

London was at its best that July evening, with perfect summer weather, lingering twilight, and a festive atmosphere pervading the city. Well-behaved crowds clustered happily outside the massive gold-tipped wrought-iron gates in front of Buckingham Palace to watch the partygoers arrive. I'm sure the guest list was impressive.

I felt like Cinderella as our chauffeured car drove us through the palace gates into the center courtyard and up to the main entrance. Evening had turned to night when we arrived shortly after nine o'clock. Pat and I had watched the Changing of the Guard in front of Buckingham Palace but had never contemplated going inside as guests. The state rooms have been opened to the public only in recent years. We had no idea of what to expect from the evening, but we felt giddy with excitement.

The low-ceilinged Entrance Hall was dimly lit and crowded. Dozens and dozens of guests politely jostled each other lining up to ascend the Grand Staircase to our left. The staircase, topped by a domed skylight and lined with ancestral portraits, led up to the long, glass-roofed Picture Gallery where Prince Charles and Diana were greeting the eight hundred guests. Once we were clear of the stairway, I had a chance to look around at the other guests, a generally sedate crowd.

My first impression was of handsome women wearing classic evening gowns and marvelous tiaras and necklaces. I imagined those heirloom diamonds and pearls coming out of the family vault or the bank safe-deposit box especially for this gala evening. The men looked dignified in tuxedos, tails, or uniforms with ribbons and medals—very English and very military. This was the British aristocracy as I'd always imagined it—the epitome of long-standing tradition, secure in its lineage and customs.

We never saw a single one of the other Americans. I had read they included Mrs. Reagan, her California friends Alfred and Betsy Bloomingdale, the American ambassador, and only three or four others besides ourselves. The only person in the entire crowd *we* knew was Diana.

In the receiving line, we gave our names to a palace dignitary who passed it on to the members of the royal family who were welcoming their hundreds of guests. Pat and I were so eager to see Diana and the line was so crowded that neither of us can remember now if we bowed and curtsied to the Queen and Prince Philip, although we must have.

I definitely had butterflies in my stomach as we moved slowly toward Prince Charles, regal in his dress uniform, and Diana, flushed and glamorous in her deep pink, ruffled taffeta gown and diamond necklace. There was just a hint of the youngster playing dress-up about her that evening—not quite grown into her new role.

I needn't have worried about our welcome. As soon as Diana spotted me, she cried out happily, "Mrs. Robertson, I'm so *glad* you're here!" and gave me a huge, spontaneous hug.

I assured her, "We wouldn't have missed this for the world!" I was touched by her genuine warmth and by her evident surprise that we'd traveled so far to share in her triumph.

She turned quickly to exclaim, "Oh Charles, look! it's

Patrick's parents from America!" and formally introduced us to the Prince of Wales. Pat bowed and I curtsied and murmured "Your Royal Highness" just to be on the safe side. Prince Charles radiated tremendous charm and graciousness. His eyes twinkled as he smiled at us. His voice was deep, warm, and resonant, as he said, "How very nice of you to have traveled so far." I loved his voice! He seemed genuinely pleased to meet us. I thought he was absolutely terrific. I was so excited for Diana, about to marry this perfect prince.

I was still anxious about our unwanted exposure in the press, so I breathlessly explained, "Diana, just one thing. If you see anything in the papers about us, please know we had nothing to do with it. The press got to my mother-in-law. Remember? You met her last spring."

Diana smiled reassuringly, "Please don't give it a thought, Mrs. Robertson." We moved on, dazzled by our first brush with royalty. The receiving line had come to a short halt during this exchange. The guests stacking up behind us must have wondered who in the world *we* were.

Pat and I were now on our own for the evening. We had hoped to see Diana later on and maybe have a short visit. We read later that she had danced early in the evening, but we never even glimpsed her again, although we looked carefully all night. We wondered why she was so conspicuously absent. It seemed such odd behavior to miss a party in her honor. We couldn't imagine what the problem might have been. She'd looked marvelous when we'd seen her earlier, so we knew she wasn't ill. We thought maybe she was experiencing pre-wedding jitters or simple exhaustion, which would have been understandable. We were concerned about her.

We learned years later from Andrew Morton's first book that she had been very much upset the previous week about having seen an engraved bracelet that Prince Charles was planning to give to Camilla Parker-Bowles. Diana knew he had delivered the present to Camilla earlier the day of the party. At lunch that same day, Diana had asked her sisters if she should call off the wedding, since Prince Charles apparently still felt an attachment to Mrs. Parker-Bowles. They told her it was too late, joking that Diana's face was already on the souvenir tea towels. Given the incredible emotions Diana must have been feeling that night, it's a miracle she'd even managed the receiving line. How brave of her to face such overwhelming doubt at her young age and still perform in public. No wonder she'd been so happy to see us, old and trusted friends.

Carrying our champagne glasses, Pat and I wandered happily through the State Apartments, a seemingly endless succession of grand and elegant reception rooms in the West Wing of the Palace. The state rooms were built in the early 1800s by John Nash and represent the same grand style and scale as other stately homes such as Blenheim Palace, which we had toured the year before. This monumental style consists of splendid, high-ceilinged rooms with formal, classical architecture—lots of columns and pilasters delineating the walls and doorways, tall windows, and elaborately carved and recessed ceilings. The columns, doorways, and windows are marble and stone, while the wood and plaster surfaces are carved and often gilded. Lush and formal velvets, silks, and brocades in jewel tones of red, blue, green, or white are used for draperies and curtains and on upholstered chairs and sofas. Huge mirrors, chandeliers, and gilded decorations add sparkle to the atmosphere, especially at night. The effect is always rich, ornate, and magnificent. These State Apartments are clearly for official ceremonies and formal entertaining, not for daily living even by the royal family. Their private apartments are in the North Wing.

I would have to say that the grandeur of the setting and the close proximity to royalty created much of the magic of that evening. The party itself was elegant, definitely traditional, and in the best possible conservative taste. There was nothing startling or trendy about this celebration.

After the receiving line had dispersed, buffet tables were set up along almost the entire one-hundred-foot length of the Picture Gallery. Guests were offered a late-evening supper of elegant finger foods, including shrimp, caviar, tiny sandwiches, and small quiches. Liveried servants passed champagne on silver trays. Chairs were placed around the walls of several rooms for those who needed a rest. Most guests remained standing as they talked to each other, nibbled on their supper, and sipped their champagne. Pat and I were too excited to do more than sample a little shrimp and caviar. As I did not want to risk spilling on my elegant gown, I ate very carefully. Despite my efforts, I did find champagne spots on the skirt the next morning.

I am an art lover and Pat is very patient, so we spent some time viewing the incredible paintings hanging on the pink brocade walls of the Picture Gallery. The royal collection is one of the finest in the entire world. I was thrilled to see paintings by Van Dyck, Rembrandt, and other European masters in a private collection, not a museum.

Next we peeked behind the scenes and laughed out loud when we saw the red and gold Throne Room being used by bustling waiters as a large butler's pantry for the buffet next door. Quite a contrast from its normal function as the site of presentations to the Queen. An orchestra was playing sedate waltz and fox-trot music in the white and gold State Ballroom, which had another red canopied pedestal with two royal thrones at one end and is normally used for investitures and state banquets. The older guests in attendance gradually drifted in here as the evening progressed. The ballroom was virtually empty at ten o'clock while people socialized and ate supper. By two o'clock everyone had wined and dined, and the dance floor was packed with tiaras and lace, uniforms and medals.

In that particular room that night, I missed the opportunity of a lifetime—the chance to talk, however briefly, with a major world leader. As Pat and I entered the ballroom, we saw Margaret Thatcher, recently elected as Prime Minister, standing alone at the edge of the dance floor. Dignified and at ease, she was calmly surveying the scene, just as we were. I couldn't believe that the most powerful woman in England, maybe the world, was being overlooked by the other guests.

I was impressed by her intelligence and resolve and by her success in reaching the top of two traditionally and strongly male bastions, the Conservative Party and the House of Commons. She was and is one of my heroines. I *should* have walked over, confidently told her how much I admired her, and let the conversation go from there. Since she was an ordinary citizen, not royalty, it would have been all right for me to speak to her. But . . . I choked.

Foolishly, I was afraid I would have trouble keeping up a stimulating conversation. I had been a mostly stay-at-home mother for several months and was feeling a bit out of touch. I was certainly not up to speed on world, let alone English, political affairs. I let the opportunity slip. Dumb, dumb, dumb. I could have asked about her children or the ball . . . anything. I can't believe I was ever so timid and unsure. Now, in my fifties, I'd walk up to anyone in the world and fearlessly start a conversation, but not back then.

As Pat and I stood there, awed by Mrs. Thatcher, we both thought of the "lonely at the top" aspect of her lofty

position. She was almost as much an outsider in that aristocratic crowd as we were. Shortly, a presentable-looking
young man, undoubtedly an aide or a bodyguard, appeared
at her side to keep her company.

Next Pat and I moved on and found more action and
louder music in the smaller, round, blue-toned Music Room,
which was set up as a discotheque with dim lights and the
usual glittering silvered globe suspended from the ceiling for
the evening. *This* dance floor was packed with the younger
guests, who looked elegant in evening dress but danced as if
they were in blue jeans. They were not wearing the jewels or
medals of the older guests, but appeared relaxed and familiar
with such elegant surroundings. As the evening went on, the
young crowd grew rowdier.

Pat is not much of a dancer and we'd nibbled already,
so we sipped our champagne and concentrated on discreet
people watching. It was fascinating.

First, we recognized Diana's mother, Mrs. Frances
Shand-Kydd, from her photograph in the newspapers. She
looked stunning in a royal blue taffeta gown. Diana's beauty
clearly came from her mother's side of the family. I felt I was
in good company, dresswise, since Diana, her mother, and
I had all chosen brightly colored, ruffled taffeta rather than
the traditional ivory lace and satin gowns worn by so many
others. Pat thought Princess Michael of Kent, tall, blonde,
and elegant in blue, was the best-looking woman at the
party.

From a mere four or five yards away, we observed Queen Elizabeth, chatting quietly in the center of one of the drawing rooms. She looked pleasant and rather motherly, wearing an ivory lace evening gown with a full skirt, her blue Order of the Garter ribbon across her chest, a diamond tiara on her head, and predictable long white gloves. This outfit looked very familiar from numerous official photographs and portraits—similar, in fact, to her coronation dress. I wondered if the queen always wore the same attire for formal occasions—a sort of royal uniform, perhaps. Pat and I smiled to see a small evening bag with a short handle hooked over her left elbow. We wondered why she would carry a handbag in her own home. What would she possibly need from it?

I was longing to walk over to Her Majesty, the Queen, and tell her, mother to mother, "Your Majesty, we've known Lady Diana quite well for the past year and a half. We'd like you to know what a truly lovely young woman your son is about to marry." A sincere and uncontroversial prewedding remark. Unfortunately, this was not only the groom's mother but also Her Majesty, the Queen of England. Protocol prevented our approaching her, since we had not been personally introduced. I toyed briefly with the idea of walking up to her anyway and pretending that, as an American, I didn't know the rules. But I was afraid of a chilling rebuff and did not want to embarrass Diana, who had been kind enough to invite us. Pat did not encourage me to plunge ahead. In fact, this time he exclaimed, "Have you lost your mind?" Maybe I should have taken a chance. Too timid again!

Our next glimpse of the royal family was Prince Philip, socializing a room or two away from the queen and surrounded by attractive women. He was a bit shorter than he appears in photographs, but quite handsome with a dignified presence and a regal, controlled charm. Pat was impressed by how flawlessly Prince Philip played his role as host, speaking graciously to people in small groups, then moving smoothly on to the next group, unhurried and polished. I thought he had an intimidating, wouldn't "suffer fools gladly" air—not a person with whom one could easily make small talk, although his close friends seemed relaxed with him. It was easy to believe that he had been a stern and domineering father to Prince Charles. The Prince of Wales had seemed much warmer and more approachable.

From time to time, Pat and I took a few moments from our people watching to stand at the tall windows thrown open to the extensive gardens lying behind the palace. We gazed out at a perfect summer night—warm, soft, and moonlit. Pure enchantment! This was a very heady experience for us—to be at Buckingham Palace . . . at a private ball given by the Queen and the Duke of Edinburgh . . . friends of the soon-to-be Princess of Wales. Pat and I said to each other again and again that evening, "Can you believe we're here? This is incredible!" As we viewed the luxury of the ball, I observed to Pat, "Well, if the Queen of England can't throw a world-class party for her son, who on earth can?"

By the early hours of the morning, everyone had loosened up and the ballroom floor was now filled with swirling gowns and shimmering jewels and medals. Pat and I even drifted onto the dance floor. A waltz seemed the right pace for this gala occasion. We were surprised to see that Princess Margaret, among others, had tied a festive balloon to her diamond tiara. Actually, there were lots of balloons bobbing in the air above the dancers.

This touch of informality and humor provided a delightful last image of the aristocracy for us to take away from the evening and remember always. By three o'clock, it was time for us to leave.

What a magical, magical night! The Cinderella feeling had lingered through the evening. This had certainly been the grandest party we would ever see.

The next day, Tuesday, Pat and I slept late, then took a leisurely stroll around our favorite residential sections of London, Hyde Park, and Saint James's Park and recalled our countless happy walks with Patrick in his stroller the previous year. It seemed so lonesome without him. We'd thought a vacation alone would be a wonderful break but were surprised to find that neither of us could wait to get home to our child, in spite of our great excitement about Diana's wedding.

So that the general public could participate in the wedding celebration, a fireworks display in Hyde Park was planned for that evening. Pat and I invited Lee Thistlethwaite, our English friend, Lee's fiancée, and Bob Sewell, an American banker friend, to Dennis's flat for drinks and snacks. Then the five of us took a short walk to Hyde Park to enjoy the fireworks with thousands of Londoners. In the midst of the happy throngs and the noise of the display, Pat and I were dragging—jet-lagged from our trip and still floating on air from the party the night before. We went to sleep around midnight to rest up for the wedding at eleven o'clock the next morning.

∞

*P*at and I were suddenly awakened by the sound of sandblasting from the house renovation next door at seven o'clock the next morning. This early wake-up gave us more than enough time to dress for the wedding. Our car and driver were arriving before nine o'clock to allow sufficient time for the long, slow drive through the crowds to Saint Paul's. Pat wore the formal morning dress that is standard attire in England for formal daytime events, such as weddings or the Ascot races. I chose a periwinkle crepe chemise and a broad-brimmed straw hat with a periwinkle ribbon I'd tied around the crown. Compared to our jitters before the ball, we were relatively calm that morning, since we would be only two guests out of two and a half thousand at the wedding. There would be no close encounters with royalty that day.

As we set out, we were pleased to see that Wednesday was another glorious summer day. We zigzagged along residential streets until we approached the two-mile carriage route from Buckingham Palace to Saint Paul's. As our car reached the access point to the procession route, we saw wooden barricades and thousands of policemen separating the roadway from the hundreds of thousands of jubilant spectators, packed twelve deep along the sidewalks and spilling out from every available window. People of all ages were milling around, waving small British flags, banners, and pictures. Many were dressed patriotically in hats or shirts of red, white, and blue. Those closest to the barriers had been waiting all night or longer for a close-up view of the procession.

The public's joy and excitement at the marriage of their prince was contagious. England, as a nation, needed this happy, binding-together event. The year 1981 had seen deepening recession, rising unemployment, civil riots, and antigovernment demonstrations. In London on that sunny July morning, there was no sign of these troubles.

As Pat and I drove along the procession route, bystanders peered into our hired limousine. They must have thought we were important guests. Of course we were not, but it was fun to feel as if we were. I wondered what it would be like to be important and famous and to travel like this, protected and isolated, all the time, as Diana soon would. Together, we tried to imagine what Diana would be feeling as she rode in the glass coach to the enthusiastic cheers of her adoring subjects. Probably thrilled and over-whelmed in equal parts.

The British public had quickly and sincerely taken the new princess-to-be to their hearts. Diana had high expecta-tions to live up to and she was still very young. She had barely turned twenty. Her birthday was July 1. I wondered if some part of the reason for the late July wedding date was so that she would be comfortably out of her teens when she mar-ried. I thought mischievously about the palace's reaction to possible headlines such as "Prince Weds Teenager."

Diana's marriage to Prince Charles was the first royal wedding ever to be held in Saint Paul's. Westminster Abbey, the traditional site for state and royal ceremonies, was not large enough to hold the 2,500 guests. Pat and I had visited Saint Paul's the previous year and seen it as an impressive public monument, filled with sightseers. That day, the cathedral came to life when it became the setting for this splendid royal ceremony.

The west front was magnificent, as always, with massive double columns and classical pediments framed by twin stone towers. Saint Paul's huge gold-topped dome is London's most visible landmark, serving as a beacon for the city since 1708. Along with the other arriving guests, Pat and I climbed the two wide flights of steps that stretch across the entire west front. That morning the steps were flanked by upright military men in full dress uniforms. As we crossed the imposing portico, we were directed to a side doorway where we presented our admission ticket to a steward.

Pat and I felt rather insignificant in a throng that included not only England's most important, famous, and titled citizens but also most of western Europe's royalty and heads of state from all over the world. The marriage of the heir to the English throne was very much a grand state occasion, in contrast to the ball, which had been a private celebration. The relative intimacy of the ball and the chance to visit with Diana made the party the more dazzling experience for us that week. Nonetheless, our spirits were buoyed by the happy fact that we actually knew the bride.

Given our lack of social or political stature, Pat and I had joked that our assigned seats were likely to be at the very back of the nave and behind a pillar. Silently, we gave each other wide-eyed looks of surprise as the usher led us slowly up and up the center aisle to seats under the famous crossing dome, less than a dozen rows from the very front of the nave. We were floored! We would have an unobstructed view of the ceremony taking place on the dais on the front edge of the choir. As we entered our row to the left, we noticed Mrs. Thatcher, somber in dark blue, on the aisle in the same row to the right. Once again, I regretted my timidity two nights earlier.

Pat and I couldn't understand how we had ended up so near to the front of the cathedral. We assumed some error had been made, but were grateful for the mistake. Years later, when I was in London for Diana's funeral, I learned that she had been allowed only one hundred personal invitations to her own wedding. We must have been in that small group, fortunately placed near the front of the church.

As we waited almost breathlessly for the ceremony to begin, Pat and I gazed discreetly at our splendid surroundings and the other guests privileged to be inside the cathedral. Once again, we didn't know a soul and we would only see Diana from a distance today.

On normal days, the spacious interior of Saint Paul's appears cool and gray, flooded with natural daylight. That day the interior positively glowed. The pillars were turned a soft honey color, as the brilliant lighting needed for television cameras and photographers reflected off the golden decoration and mosaics of the ceiling domes. The air was filled with the rich sound of stately music, the rustle of elegant dresses, and the whisper of hundreds of muted conversations. Saint Paul's was alive with pageantry and excitement.

In the congregation around us, we saw hundreds and hundreds of women in hats and elegant short dresses in summer-bright shades of red, blue, and yellow or pastel tones of pink, lavender, azure, and cream. The men wore formal light or dark gray morning suits or dress uniforms and were hatless in church. The famous Beefeater guards, striking in the red uniforms with white ruffs normally seen at the Tower of London, stood around the perimeter of the summer-hued throng. Cameramen were stationed upon beige-covered platforms attached to the crossing pillars or were perched on scaffolding high up along the walls. A second choir and small orchestra was arrayed in front of the doorway of the north transept to our left. The anticipation and goodwill inside the church were palpable but well controlled—a great contrast to the open exuberance we had seen and heard on the streets.

Shortly before eleven o'clock, the members of the Spencer family followed by the Queen and the royal family walked to the measured pace of processional music up the red-carpeted center aisle. The Spencers were seated to the left of the dais, the Windsors to the right. Then the proceedings moved into high gear.

The cheerful trumpet strains of Purcell's "Prince of Denmark March" sang out as Prince Charles, flanked by Princes Andrew and Edward, strode confidently up the aisle, smiling and nodding to his friends in the congregation. He seemed very much at ease as he took his place to await his bride.

Then . . . we heard the trumpet fanfare that heralded Diana's entrance. We could not see her arrival from our seats to the side. Very clearly, though, we could hear the murmurs and gasps of approval inside the church along with the cheers and applause outside, as the entire world first glimpsed the bride in her fairy-tale dress.

Diana looked an absolute vision in her cloud of tulle, taffeta, and lace, with the Spencer diamond tiara sparkling above her veil. Lovely, innocent, and demure, she more than met her subjects' expectations that glorious morning.

Holding her father's arm, Diana progressed slowly and beautifully up the aisle to the rustle of silk and the scrutiny of the congregation. I recognized the processional march as Jeremiah Clarke's "Trumpet Voluntary" from my own wedding. She appeared outwardly composed, almost deadly calm, with an endearing tentative quality to her smile. I felt certain she was trembling inside. I was quaking in sympathy for her.

It may have been simply the effect of the artificial light, but I thought Diana looked rather pale and tense under her veil. Even Pat noticed. He turned to me and whispered, "She looks as nervous as you did, almost green around the gills." I definitely agreed. Diana had looked happier, healthier, fresher the previous year and the night of the ball. The strain of recent events was telling on her. We supposed it to be the excessive prewedding stress—simply too much pressure at one time for so young a bride.

I know mine is a minority view, but I would have preferred a simpler wedding gown on Diana. I thought the ruffles, poufs, and bows drew too much attention to the dress and not enough to the naturally lovely, graceful bride. Still, the overall effect of the intricate design and sumptuous fabric on Diana was marvelous.

Pat and I listened attentively to the ceremony and wiped at our tears when Prince Charles and Diana exchanged the traditional vows. We both sniffle at weddings, probably because we remember our own and we're still so happy with each other. We viewed getting married as a very private commitment.

We marveled at Diana's poise as she took her wedding vows, surrounded by thousands of strangers in Saint Paul's and watched by hundreds of millions of television viewers around the world. In the occasional moments of silence between prayers, hymns, and vows, we could hear the whirring of television cameras and the clicking of still photography.

I breathed a sigh of relief once the mutual pledge of vows was over. At this point, stewards brought up red and gold benches so the new couple could sit down as the ceremony continued. Prince Charles and Diana also seemed relieved to have completed the critical part of the proceedings. We could see them smile at each other and exchange quiet comments to relieve the tension.

The next part of the ceremony included several moments that were touching on that day and that seem poignant, even wrenching, from my perspective today. The then-speaker of the House of Commons read from Paul's First Letter to the Corinthians about faith, hope, and love. I was to hear Prime Minister Tony Blair read this famous New Testament passage with greater relevance at Diana's funeral sixteen years later. Then the Archbishop of Canterbury began his homily with the often-quoted opening, "Here is the stuff of which fairy tales are made." That morning we all believed the magic to be true.

Next the Archbishop led the bride and groom to the altar for more prayers and hymns. These included "The Lord's Prayer," in which the congregation joined, and "I Vow to Thee My Country," the hymn chosen by Diana for her wedding and by her son William for her funeral, far too soon after her wedding.

A lengthy break in the ceremony occurred as Prince Charles and Diana and members of both their families went off to a side aisle to sign the official registers. Kiri Te Kanawa, the world famous Maori soprano, sang Handel's "Let the Bright Seraphim" to a trumpet accompaniment, followed by more choral music. At this point, my thoughts turned again to Diana.

Pat and I were there only because our gentle, innocent, unassuming nanny was being married that day. The splendid pageantry, the glittering guest list, the long-awaited wedding dress were all very much secondary considerations. We were thrilled, of course, to be included in this once-in-a-lifetime event, but we would have traveled to our nanny's wedding if she'd been Diana Jones marrying a bank clerk in the suburbs. Our *only* concern that day was Diana. Would she be happy? We thought so then. Although I couldn't imagine that they wouldn't live happily ever after, I prayed a silent little prayer for Diana's future.

Finally, the royal newlyweds faced the congregation together for the first time and stepped down toward the center aisle, pausing to bow and curtsy to the Queen. One of

Elgar's more joyous marches resounded throughout the cathedral as the bride and groom, smiling and happy, moved down the aisle. I was hoping desperately that we would catch her eye for an instant, as we were only a few seats in from the aisle. She was walking on our side of the church, but she never glanced in our direction. This was such a grand occasion, there was no way we could gesture to catch her eye. It was so frustrating not to be able to communicate our joy.

As we waited inside for our turn to leave, we could hear the cheers and applause break out in the streets as the prince and princess emerged for their ride back to the palace. The bells of Saint Paul's rang out, proclaiming the royal marriage. Our hearts were bursting with pride and happiness for Diana.

The wedding had been a magnificent ritual, flawlessly orchestrated. A deeply moving personal event, as well as a splendid state occasion—a royal pageant on a scale that the British execute better than anyone in the world. As Pat and I joined the exuberant crowds outside, we were struck again by the public's spontaneous, joyful response to their new princess.

On that glorious, sunny July day, all of us—the thousands of guests in the congregation, the hundreds of thousands of people on the streets of London, the hundreds of millions of television viewers around the world, and most of all, Diana herself—believed in the fairy tale.

∞

*A*fter the excitement and glamour of the wedding, Pat and I both experienced a postcelebration letdown, but we were happy to get home to Patrick. I settled once again into what became the pattern of my life for the next ten years—parenting, arranging play dates and car pools, running my household, paying the bills, doing volunteer work in the community and part-time consulting work for David. Normally I worked on my financial reports at home in the evenings and on weekends when Pat could look after Patrick, and later Caroline, if he was not traveling overseas for Exxon.

Since 1980 we have moved seven times with Pat's job. Each time, I promptly wrote to Diana with our new address. For sixteen years, she never missed a move. Nevertheless, I worried each time that our address change would get lost in the mountains of mail at Buckingham Palace.

As soon as Diana returned from her honeymoon, she sent us a photograph of her wedding party and a brief note sending her love. For years, Diana and I wrote to each other regularly. And every Christmas through 1996, Diana sent us personally signed Christmas cards with beautiful photographs and loving greetings.

Diana's letters were spontaneous and written quickly with an occasional spelling or grammatical mistake or a crossed-out correction, which was endearing. She used a looped addition sign for "and," dashes instead of periods to quickly connect ideas, underlining for emphasis, and lots of exclamation marks to express enthusiasm and heartfelt feelings. Next to her signature, she used her distinctive hugs-and-kisses symbol—an X for a kiss enclosed in a circle for a hug. Her handwriting mirrored her personality—open, warm, and generous. I assumed her life was happy and stable. Her letters gave no hint to the contrary. I did not realize, at least in the early years, that my letters were probably a welcome reminder of a happier, simpler time in her life.

At first, it was intimidating to write to her not as "Diana" but as "Her Royal Highness, Princess of Wales." I marked my letters "Personal" or "Confidential" and mailed them with certified and return receipt requested forms to ensure that they would arrive at Buckingham Palace. After that, the palace's internal system would determine if my letters reached Diana. The local postal clerks always looked at me curiously when they noticed the address on my envelopes. I began my letters with the greeting "Your Royal Highness." I had to observe the right protocol. If her staff opened or screened her letters, they would expect recognition of her royal position. I never asked Diana if she cared about the use of her title. Once I got past the formal address and greeting, I would think "Dear Diana" and write about our various family pursuits as well as my reactions to what I had read about her in the press.

I did my best to keep up with the events in her life. I devoured press articles about her, but only those in the reputable news magazines. I bought a few of the picture books about Diana, especially if they contained the news photos of Diana pushing Patrick in his stroller. She photographed so beautifully that it was a joy to look at her pictures. At bookstores, I scanned some of the early biographies, but quickly spotted so many inaccuracies just based on my personal knowledge that I never bought a single one. I am not a celebrity watcher. I would never have followed Diana in the press so carefully if I had not known her.

I worked to make my letters newsy, cheerful, and well informed about her life so that Diana would look forward to receiving them. She knew that I was genuinely sympathetic and encouraging, especially in the later years as news of her problems gradually, then openly, emerged.

The tone of our letters followed the pattern Diana and I

had set when she was Patrick's nanny—personal, honest, and caring, but never intrusive or overly familiar. Positive and supportive, but never fawning or effusive. I would write one or two drafts of each letter to make sure my words struck the right note. I was careful to use full titles if I mentioned "Her Majesty, the Queen" or "His Royal Highness, Prince of Wales," in case her husband or her staff saw my letters. When I wrote about her children, I felt more comfortable and usually referred to "your boys" or "your sons."

While Patrick was young and accompanied me on my errands, he and I would often spot Diana's photograph smiling out from magazine covers as we waited in the grocery-store checkout line. At two and a half, Patrick recognized her beautiful face from the framed pictures we had at home. He would point excitedly, as if to say, "There's Diana!", with no conception of why we were seeing her familiar face so often. I'm sure the other shoppers assumed we were simply distant fans. We kept the fact that we actually knew the most photographed woman in the world a closely held secret as we moved around with Pat's job. We especially did not want to draw any notice from the press as Diana became more famous. We'd experienced enough media attention just before her wedding. Only our oldest friends and our families knew about our friendship.

In May of 1982 as Diana waited for her first child to arrive, she sent an especially warm and confiding letter in response to one I had just written. First, she wrote "Please never stop writing. . . ." And I never did, although there were times when my letter writing became sporadic. She expressed the wonderment familiar to new mothers-to-be: "It seems amazing that in six weeks we will be three and a lot of fuss is starting. . . ." As a result, she expressed a strong protective instinct for her child: "I feel that the baby would be much safer and protected if it stayed inside me!" She mentioned a much needed holiday in Eleuthera, adding, "Unfortunately the press wouldn't leave us alone, so that was rather sad. . . ." She sounded so wistful and tolerant toward the press at that time. The vacation did give her "the opportunity of being alone with my husband for a change!"

I had written that Patrick always recognized her picture in the press. She responded, "It's very touching to know that he recognizes me." Diana had been interviewing experienced, adult nannies for her child and had found one she liked. She only hoped that the nanny wouldn't take too much control over the nursery. Diana was so very young that her concern was natural. At least, I thought, Diana would not have to worry about neglect or abuse of her child, as I did when I first looked for a caretaker for Patrick. I had imagined every horrible possibility as I started to interview people and really worked myself into a state. Thankfully, Patrick had only affectionate and devoted caretakers. It is ironic that the more competently a nanny does her job, the more inadequate a new mother can feel.

Diana went on to confess that she had been feeling quite sick throughout her pregnancy. I was aware of the strain of her public engagements but not of her other health or marital problems. I had been lucky to have a very good pregnancy with Patrick at thirty-five. I felt sorry for her physical distress. She noted gamely that she has been "assured that it's all worth while!" She certainly knew that I thought so.

Diana closed with an unexpected but welcome invitation. If we could come to England, she wrote, "I'd love to see you and introduce you to my wonderful husband!!" She must have forgotten that we'd met him briefly at the prenuptial ball. I wondered when, or even if, she would realize that like all husbands, Prince Charles was less than perfect. Did a royal princess ever have to come down to earth as the rest of us eventually do in our less glamorous marriages?

I was unable to visit Diana in those early years. Patrick was a restless traveler, so bringing him on a seven-hour flight would have been too exhausting, along with the jet lag. But I could never have left him at home. Diana certainly wanted to see him, in fact, probably more than she wanted to see me. The expense of airplane tickets and a hotel was also a problem. We had a very tight budget with our first house and child on one salary, particularly since we'd originally planned on my working. Money was obviously never an issue for Diana, but I expect she would have understood my problems with time, distance, and expense had I ever mentioned them. Now I desperately wish I'd tried to visit more often, but I thought we had decades ahead of us.

Six weeks later on June 21, 1982, Diana's first son, William, was born to tremendous fanfare and celebration. Diana had not even turned twenty-one. She became a princess, wife, and mother all in her twentieth year. At that age I was still in college, studying history and art and dating boys from Harvard and Dartmouth. In her role as Princess of Wales, Diana normally interacted with adults older than herself. At times she would "yearn for my age group." Her old friends told her she had not changed at all, except to grow up, which she observed was "needed." To me, twenty-one still seemed awfully young for all her responsibilities.

We sent Diana and Prince William our favorite bedtime books, *Goodnight, Moon* and *Runaway Bunny*, both by Margaret Wise Brown. I remembered how Diana had loved reading daytime nursery-rhyme books to Patrick. I felt she would actually use and enjoy these extraordinarily tender books. The soothing words and images in *Goodnight, Moon* will help to put even the most wakeful child to sleep. *Runaway Bunny* is a beautiful and simple story of motherly love. I had been touched when Patrick, at two and a half, explained that the story was about "you and me."

Diana wrote in September to thank me for the two books. She emphasized their "extreme happiness and contentment" and said that she and Prince Charles were "gaga and adoring" parents. She admitted that she was exhausted and trying hard to cope with "this small parcel!" Again, her honesty and good nature showed. With hindsight, this was an enormous understatement. I read many years later that she had suffered badly from postpartum depression. I had endured only one very long day of the baby blues after Patrick's birth. I cannot imagine Diana feeling that unhappy for weeks at a time when she was supposed to be glowing with the joys of new motherhood. She was sensible and down to earth about her son from the start, writing that her son had received "a mass of presents giving William such a spoiling start to his life—" It seemed that the public's excitement over Prince William's birth had taken both his parents by surprise. With this letter Diana enclosed a signed photograph of herself with her infant son and wrote "hopefully you might like to have it—" Again, that endearing modesty.

The following spring on May 9, 1983, my daughter, Caroline, was born—a perfect, happy, healthy baby, even though I was a month away from my fortieth birthday. Patrick had been very happy as an only child for four years and did not welcome his sister's arrival. I wondered if I had the patience and stamina to cope with two small children. Also that summer, Pat's job required us to move to New Jersey from Bronxville, where I had been very happy. It was a very wearing summer for me. One bright spot that July was the short, sweet note of congratulations that Diana sent along with a little cardigan decorated with bunnies for my new daughter.

Diana wrote again in January 1984 and described Christmas with her eight-month-old son. "William . . . was into every parcel like a whirlwind, leaving his parents exhausted!" In response to my writing that I hoped to manage a trip to England with Patrick in June, Diana wrote "please make a space for us as I'd love to show you my little man as well as see Patrick!" She seemed eager to remain friends. I was amazed and touched.

That spring I wrote to give Diana our travel dates. She replied in mid-April with her schedule for June, saying "both William and I . . . would love to see you and Patrick if it's possible." Diana's second child was now on the way, due that September. A week after I received her letter, we learned that Exxon was transferring us to Houston that summer, less than a year after we'd moved to New Jersey. This meant that in June I would be packing up for a long-distance move, not traveling to London to visit Diana. The combined stresses of two young children, part-time work, looking for a new house and a kindergarten for Patrick in Houston, and packing and selling the house in New Jersey were too much for me. Pat had already been sent on ahead to his new assignment. I simply couldn't cope with a transatlantic trip—no matter how much I wanted to see Diana. Missing that visit was a huge disappointment.

Diana's second son, Prince Harry, was born on September 15, 1984, at the same time that Patrick was entering kindergarten in Houston. I cannot find a thank-you note from Diana, so I must have been too frazzled to send a present for Prince Harry's arrival.

That fall I was struggling with a second move in less than a year, major renovation on our house, life in a sprawling, congested city that I soon learned to love, and physical exhaustion because Caroline never slept. Diana also had two young children along with her official duties and travel. At least she had excellent help. I had none at all. Neither of us was a good correspondent that year, except for our Christmas cards.

∞

*I*n September 1985, Judy Paine, one of my closest friends and a devoted admirer of the Princess of Wales, called from New Orleans to tell me that Prince Charles and Diana were scheduled to stop in Washington, D.C., in November as part of a world tour. I had not yet read of their impending visit. Never one to hesitate, Judy urged me to write to Diana and to ask if Patrick and I could visit her in the capital. Judy also suggested that I say Patrick and I were already planning to visit friends in Washington that same week, so a visit with Diana would be very easy for us to arrange. This was not exactly true, but I thought mentioning this coincidence would not hurt our chances. At this time, I had apparently forgotten Diana's earlier invitations to visit her in London or I would not have been so tentative about writing. Since I've always kept her letters and cards in a bank safe-deposit box, they were not readily accessible as a reminder.

I was not optimistic about receiving any response to my letter, let alone a positive one. By that time Diana had become a full-fledged celebrity. She and Prince Charles were already the most talked-about couple in the world, and this world tour was increasing their exposure even more. I waited with very little hope of a reply.

I was amazed to receive a letter dated October 4 from Sarah Gillett at the British embassy in Washington, telling me that "the Princess of Wales would very much like to see you both." The letter invited Patrick and me to attend an outdoor reception and tree-planting ceremony on Saturday, November 9, at 12:15, "after which there would be an opportunity for you to see the Princess of Wales privately in the Residence."

I stared at the embassy letter in stunned disbelief. I had never expected private time with Diana but rather a quick hug and hello in a receiving line similar to our encounter at the ball at Buckingham Palace. I called Ms. Gillett immediately to reply and to verify that Patrick and I were, indeed, to have a private audience with our famous nanny. It just seemed too good to be true!

Next I hurried to make plane and hotel reservations and to buy dress clothes for Patrick, who was now six. He did not particularly enjoy the shopping expedition, as we bought him a very traditional outfit—navy blazer, blue button-down shirt, dark tie and socks, gray flannel slacks, and dark brown loafers. I planned to wear a dark silk dress and burgundy wool jacket I already had in the closet. I remembered that Diana had complimented me on that color in London years ago. Caroline was too young and rambunctious as a two-year-old to bring to a formal visit at the embassy, so she stayed home with her dad, who took time off from work to baby-sit. I had not even asked to include Pat and Caroline when I wrote to Diana. I did not want my request to be too cumbersome by inviting all four of us. The friendship was really between Diana and me, mother to mother, with Patrick as the common link.

Two complications arose before we flew to Washington. First, Judy asked if I would see if Adrienne, her fourteen-year-old daughter, could be included in our visit, possibly as Patrick's current baby-sitter. Adrienne idolized Diana and was dying for a glimpse of her in person. I have always been very fond of Adrienne, so I called Ms. Gillett at the embassy and received permission to take Adrienne along. Second, I developed a bad sore throat and severe laryngitis. I had been caught in a heavy rainstorm while helping out at a children's Halloween party and still had a deep, scratchy voice more than a month later.

The Monday before we left on our trip, I wrote a note to Bonnie Clarke, Patrick's teacher, telling her Patrick would be missing school on Friday, November 8. I said only that we would be visiting friends in Washington. While Patrick waited in the car-pool line, Mrs. Clarke had asked him whom he was going to see, expecting him to name cousins or other relatives. He had replied, "My mom and I are going to visit Diana." When I arrived, Mrs. Clarke said, "This is so cute. You won't believe what Patrick just told me. He said you two were going to see Diana. It couldn't possibly be true!" Patrick and I both thought Mrs. Clarke was an exceptional teacher, but I was a little miffed that she would think he was fibbing. While I normally never talked about Diana, I couldn't let this pass. I explained, "Patrick never lies. We are, in fact, going to visit Diana. She was his nanny when we lived in London." Mrs. Clarke apologized quickly and exclaimed, "Oh! So you're that American family. I had no idea." Our last name is certainly common enough. The other teachers and mothers within earshot all shared in the surprise at our small connection with royalty.

On Friday, November 8, Patrick and I met Adrienne at National Airport and we took a taxi to the Ritz Carlton, which had very reasonable rates on the weekends and was convenient to the British ambassador's residence. The three of us had an early supper at the Old Ebbitt Grill near the White House, then went to bed early to rest up for our important day. We stayed together in one big room, with Patrick snuggled next to me in a king-size bed and Adrienne on a foldout sofa. Adrienne's mom did not want her young daughter staying alone in a hotel. The youngsters slept soundly. I was too excited to sleep much.

It wasn't that I was nervous about seeing Diana again. I felt certain she and I would pick up where we had left off in our letters and would soon be talking comfortably about our children. And I knew she would dote upon Patrick. But I was apprehensive about the setting and the entourage we would encounter before we saw Diana alone. Meeting with royalty, even if she's been one's nanny, is definitely an awesome experience.

The British Embassy very kindly sent a chauffeured car to collect us at our hotel. At the last minute, I had quickly emptied my small dressy purse and popped in my Kodak Instamatic camera, in the hope that I could manage a picture of Patrick with Diana. Adrienne helped me carry the large, brightly wrapped toys we'd brought along for Diana's boys.

We felt very pampered as we rode in the embassy limousine through Rock Creek Park and down elegant streets lined with large, well-landscaped homes. It was a glorious fall day. Washington looked particularly beautiful with the trees turning yellow and orange and red in the midday sunlight. As we turned into the residence, we had a quick glimpse of the imposing, beautifully proportioned, soft red-brick mansion surrounded by acres of immaculately maintained grounds. The limousine swept under a low, covered portico where we were met by Ms. Gillett, who had arranged our visit. She led us inside up a wide, shallow stairway of austere, cool gray stone and out into an enormous garden.

There, Patrick, Adrienne, and I joined the embassy staff and hundreds of guests standing behind temporary fencing and waiting eagerly for Prince Charles and Diana to begin their handshaking "walkabout." We heard sighs of delight and admiration as Prince Charles and Diana, dazzling in bright red, emerged from the French doors of the residence.

The slim, grown-up, glamorous Diana I spied over the heads of the crowd bore no resemblance to our shy teenage nanny. Of course, I'd seen countless photographs in the press, but here she was—the real person—before my eyes. I was spellbound as I watched her from a short distance. Her lovely smile and glowing presence captivated all of us. Diana did not see us in the dense crowd. Patrick and I had stayed back, knowing we'd meet her inside shortly. Adrienne squeezed her way to the front row to see her dream princess up close and maybe shake her royal hand.

While the couple planted a commemorative tree, Patrick, Adrienne, and I were escorted back into the residence to await Diana. Despite my assurances about Adrienne's devotion, Anne Beckwith-Smith, Diana's private secretary at that time, deftly and swiftly pulled her away to wait elsewhere. Frankly, I don't think Diana would have objected if Adrienne had been included.

Patrick and I stood waiting in the terrifically grand central hallway of the residence. Marble columns stretched up almost out of sight, at least thirty feet up to the ceiling. The hallway was spacious and light-filled, with tall windows and French doors along one side and an enormous reception or dining room on the other. The residence appeared to come from the same era as Buckingham and Blenheim Palaces—grand, ornate, and formal—but the residence seemed airier, lighter, and prettier. I thought it was the most beautiful building I'd ever been inside. From time to time, I've recalled this tiny glimpse of how the rich and important live.

While we waited, Patrick and I chatted quietly with Ambassador and Lady Wight, who were dignified but very natural and gracious at the same time. The three grown-ups engaged in polite small talk about the royal visit, the weather, Diana, and our connection with her. Patrick appeared as cool as a little cucumber, answered the Wights' questions politely, and patted their large friendly yellow Labradors. He was so calm and collected that the Wights commented enthusiastically on his poise and manners. I was so proud of him I could have burst! No wonder he was calm. He was eager to see the person he knew only as his former nanny. My heart had started thumping with antici-pation. So much had changed in Diana's life. This would be our first meeting since she had become the Princess of Wales and a celebrity. Would she still be the same Diana underneath? Based on her letters, I thought so.

Next Patrick and I were shown into the library, a warmer room with high ceilings and sunlight flooding in from tall windows. Carved wooden bookcases, glowing with a centuries-old patina, lined the walls and held leather-bound, gilt-edged volumes. I loved this room. I wished I could have leafed through a few of those beautiful old books. I was calmer now, prepared for a cozy mother-to-mother visit with Diana. Patrick and I stood expectantly in the center of the elegant room. I rested my right arm around his little shoulders. I needed the support more than he did.

Then the door opened and Diana entered ... with Prince Charles. I held my breath as she gave us a brilliant smile and briskly crossed the floor.

The new Diana was truly breathtaking—beautiful, self-assured, polished, and stunning in her scarlet suit. She looked even more radiant in person than in her best pictures. She was absolute perfection, with her flawless complexion, starry blue eyes, and confident carriage. A remarkable and complete transformation from young nanny to global sensation—and she was only twenty-four!

Before either one of us said a word, Diana and I exchanged glances for just an instant. I didn't even try to hide my amazement and admiration. My eyes and smile said, "Wow! I'm speechless." Diana's impish grin replied, "Yes, I've done pretty well, haven't I?" It was an unforgettable, private moment.

I had not expected to see Prince Charles. I had done a double take as he entered, and I could feel my knees actually knocking together as he walked over to us. I was terrified at the prospect of carrying on a personal conversation with the man born to be king of England. This was not going to be a quick curtsy in a receiving line. I can still feel my total panic when I recall that encounter now. That afternoon he looked a great deal more informal than when Pat and I had met him in his full dress uniform at the ball. He wore an impeccably tailored dark suit with a light blue shirt and pale pink tie. For a few seconds I was utterly flustered. I didn't know what to do first—curtsy, say "hello," introduce Patrick to the prince, or just wait.

Since Prince Charles was present, I curtsied and Patrick bowed to Diana, who impulsively hugged each of us, then introduced us to her husband. "Charles, you remember Mrs. Robertson, and of course, this is Patrick." She was beaming at my son. I curtsied to the prince and murmured, "Your Royal Highness," and Patrick bowed a second time. We'd practiced our gestures at home in front of a mirror. Charles greeted us with a gracious smile and said, "So this is Patrick! I'm delighted to see you both." His voice was deep, reassuring, and warm—definitely one of his most attractive features.

We were still standing in the middle of the room as I told them how happy we were to see them. I suddenly became aware of my deep, raspy voice. I said, "I'm so sorry. I know this sounds dreadful," and explained that I'd developed the laryngitis from getting caught in the rain.

Prince Charles immediately chuckled, "Don't worry. I

think it sounds very sexy." We all laughed. His funny, spontaneous compliment put me at ease. Then I told Diana how much I treasured her letters and Christmas cards and her continuing friendship. I stressed, "All your correspondence is safely tucked away at our bank. Please know that we have never talked about you to the press."

Again Charles smiled and laughed, "You must be the only person we know who hasn't!" I thought to myself, "What a darling! This is going to be all right, after all." Now I felt completely comfortable with Diana's husband, even though I did have to call him "Sir." Royal privacy was a rather sensitive issue that fall. A former valet of Prince Charles had just published a revealing memoir of his experiences in the royal household.

The four of us walked over to a pair of sofas facing each other across a low table where Cokes and orange juice had been laid out on a silver tray. Diana held Patrick's hand and settled him on the sofa between herself and her husband. I sat facing them and the closed door to the hallway beyond. We all had a cool drink and continued to talk.

I could hardly believe my eyes as I watched Patrick nestled on the sofa between the most famous couple in the world. As I carried on my conversation with the royal pair, I kept thinking, "I can't believe this! I simply can't believe this!"

We talked initially about the rigors of air travel and jet lag. Charles and Diana had just flown in from Australia that morning. Even flying by the most direct route, that trip takes twenty-four hours and stretches across sixteen time zones. They must have been exhausted, but the fatigue didn't show a bit. In particular, Diana said that she had trouble sleeping on an airplane, even a royal jet. They explained that they had been seeing people since their arrival and were due at the White House that evening, with no time to rest in between. I was exhausted simply listening to their schedule. Their glamorous trip sounded like real work to me.

In response to my query, "How in the world do you manage to keep going?" Diana admitted that the hassle of long-distance travel and frequent stops was greatly eased by having a staff to pack, unpack, and press their clothes and groom them for their many public appearances. I could easily grasp that Prince Charles and Diana could never look and act their best on short notice and little sleep without massive behind-the-scenes support.

I had never before thought about the complex inner workings of the royals' official duties. I found this glance into their world fascinating. I couldn't help contrasting Diana's elaborate travel arrangements with my own. I'd made our plane and hotel reservations, packed for both of us, traveled coach class, carried both suitcases, hailed taxis, done my own hair and makeup, and so on. I would gladly have traded places with Diana.

Charles and Diana seemed very amicable together, even joking mildly about wanting a girl "the next time," after their two boys. This topic came up because I already had my daughter. If their marriage was over by the time their second son was born in September of 1984, as each of them claimed after their 1992 separation, they certainly had me fooled. But then, I wasn't looking for any signs of discord.

Our presents for Princes William and Harry had been placed on the table earlier by a staff member. I cannot recall so many years later which particular toys we'd selected. I do know that we had chosen them on the basis of Patrick's favorites when he was younger. Diana expressed her delight at our thoughtfulness and left the toys to be unwrapped by their sons at home. I'm sure their staff was less than happy to have to transport the colorful but bulky packages back to London.

Soon the pattern of the conversation shifted a bit. Charles smiled down at Patrick and asked him about his school and sports interests. They both liked soccer. For the balance of our visit, Prince Charles and my son talked mainly to each other. I could not hear what they were saying, but I could see that the conversation seemed to be flowing smoothly. I would give anything to know what Patrick and Charles had to say to each other. Patrick was very vague when I asked him later. He had enjoyed his visit with His Royal Highness but was too young to have any idea how important Prince Charles was. I was truly touched by the prince's patience and kindness in entertaining a small child on such a hectic day. I've never forgotten what a wonderful impression he made on me that after-noon.

Diana talked directly to me about her children—her tremendous love for her boys, only one and three and a half now, and the strain of leaving them for official duties, like this world tour. She had been away for more than two weeks and couldn't wait to get home to see her sons. I sympathized with her longing. I reminded her of how much I'd missed Patrick after only eight hours at the office that year in London. We discussed nannies and the pangs of leaving one's children with others and dealing with differences in values and discipline. I believe that she'd switched nannies once by this time. Diana clearly felt that children need lots of love and hugs. I had observed this firsthand with Patrick in 1980.

I realized that Diana was very much a working mother. Certainly she had more glamorous duties and a better staff, but she was still subject to the same fatigue and the same conflicts between work and home as the rest of us. In her case, the lengthy and far-flung travel must have been especially hard to bear. Nonetheless, I imagined that luxurious surroundings and the best help available would make it easier to cope with the multiple demands on her.

Very thoughtfully Diana asked me how I was coping with "moving houses" so often and working part-time. I admitted that it was a real struggle, especially since finding good child care had proven to be virtually impossible. I told her the positive side of the chaos was that I could work at home and raise my children day to day. No separation pangs for me, just incredible fatigue. When she asked about Patrick's latest accomplishments, I proudly told her about his early reading and math skills. I also related what a little handful Caroline was turning out to be, so that she wouldn't think a baby daughter would be any easier to raise than her boys.

Diana and I soon reestablished our friendly, child-centered relationship. It was reassuring to sense the genuine warmth and kindness I'd known in 1980. The outer person had changed beyond all recognition. Diana had blossomed from a naive, unaffected teenager into a stunning, poised adult. I was particularly struck by how chatty and outgoing she had become. Not a trace of shyness left. This remarkable transformation was almost impossible for me to absorb, given my early experience with her. What neither of us knew at the time was that this initial step onto the world stage was only the beginning of her brilliant and lonely rise to fame.

At this point, I gathered up my courage and asked if they would mind if I took a picture of Patrick sitting between them. I stressed, "This is only for our family album." They smiled at each other, shrugged their shoulders, and laughed. "No, we don't mind at all." They appeared so relaxed and accommodating. This friendly visit was probably the most stress-free appearance they had made on that world tour.

As I mentioned earlier, Diana, Charles, and Patrick were seated with their backs to the library door. As I aimed my camera, I noticed a staff member peering through a small gap in the double door. I assumed it was Ms. Beckwith-Smith wishing to wind up this unofficial visit. I could visualize her with her arms crossed, tapping her foot and fuming with impatience. Charles and Diana clearly had other appointments that afternoon. Fortunately for Patrick and me, they could not see this ominous figure in the background and stayed with us for close to forty-five minutes. The couple never showed how tired they must have been or how tightly planned their schedule was. They gave the impression they would have been happy to spend the whole afternoon with us.

Diana's pleasure at seeing us was genuine, I know. Prince Charles seemed sincerely gracious, possibly the result of years of practice in putting people at ease in all situations. I prefer to believe that he is truly kind and courteous. I did wonder how Diana had managed to get him to join our visit. Surely there were more important people he could have been seeing. I marveled the entire time at their effortless manners and charm, as well as Patrick's and my complete comfort—such a contrast to my nerves before we actually met them. Given what I read years later about the escalating problems in their marriage, their friendly and unaffected manner was remarkable—the result of generations of breeding and years of training. I never guessed anything was wrong.

Finally, Ms. Beckwith-Smith entered the room to shepherd the royal couple to their next engagement. After seeing her in action earlier when she had pulled Adrienne away so firmly, I murmured to Prince Charles, "Ah, the redoubtable Miss Beckwith-Smith, again." He lifted his eyebrows in good-humored surprise and laughed wryly, "Yes. That certainly describes her." Another private joke with the Prince of Wales. I was thrilled.

As we walked back into the hallway, Patrick held on to Diana's hand. He was reluctant to let her go and gazed up at her with open adoration. I wish I could have taken another picture of that touching moment. With the royal staff clustering around, that was impossible. Diana seemed equally hesitant to say good-bye and bent down to squeeze Patrick tightly as we left. To Patrick that afternoon, Diana was truly a fairy-tale princess. Is it possible to imagine how her own sons felt about her?

I was tremendously proud of Patrick for being so poised and polite, so natural all afternoon. "God bless him," I thought. "If he ever had to be on his best behavior, it was today, when it mattered so very much." I was also feeling blissful, really floating on air, after our long and private visit with Diana and Charles. It was hard to believe that they had spent so much time with us that afternoon and later were heading to the White House to spend the evening with President and Mrs. Reagan and lots of celebrities. The often-seen photograph of Diana in a midnight blue evening gown dancing with John Travolta was taken that night.

On the taxi ride back to our hotel, we saw Diana and Charles's limousine and security escort crossing an intersection in the distance. Our taxi driver explained to us that many streets in Washington were blocked off that day due to the important state visit of the Prince and Princess of Wales. Patrick, Adrienne, and I didn't say a word. We just smiled and kept our visit a secret among ourselves. We all flew home later that afternoon.

Ten days later I was amazed to receive a letter from Diana written just days after she'd arrived home—in fact, before I'd written her a thank-you letter. I was mortified by my delay in writing to her. I had managed to fire off proper thank-you notes to Ambassador Wight and Ms. Gillett, but I had so much more to say to Diana.

Her letter was the most heartwarming one I have ever received—even more so, now that I know what personal strain she was under then. After thanking us "a *million* times" for coming to see them in Washington, she wrote, "From the beginning to the end I had a lump in my throat looking at what a special little man Patrick had grown up to be—Goodness, you must be extremely proud of him and if either of my boys turn out like Patrick I will have no worries and I *really* mean every word." I had a lump in *my* throat as I read this. I *was* very proud of Patrick and deeply touched by Diana's praise.

Diana added that, for her, the high point of the visit to

Washington was seeing Patrick and me. She explained, "Being able to get in touch with a v. happy and memorable part of my past meant a tremendous amount to me and kept me going for days!" Seeing the world-famous Diana in such a warm and personal way after five years and realizing how much she still cherished our friendship kept me going for months, even years!

∞

*I*t took weeks for me to come back to earth after seeing Diana in her glamorous royal life. I daydreamed about her world—living in palaces, traveling in limousines and private jets, having a well-trained staff to perform every mundane task, looking fabulous all the time, enjoying the adoration of crowds everywhere she went. For months, even years, I envied Diana her fairy-tale life of luxury and fame. As I folded our laundry, made the beds, loaded the dishwasher, or stood in line at the grocery store, I would think, "Diana never has to do this." I knew this was a totally irrational comparison, but I couldn't help myself. I saw her likeness on magazine covers constantly, and the memory of that extraordinary visit at the British embassy lingered.

The comparison was even more striking, since our

family was going through a particularly stressful period during early 1986. Exxon had just announced huge staff cutbacks—approximately one-third of its worldwide workforce of 150,000. We might not know for months if Pat still had a job. He wasn't worried, but the uncertainty gnawed away at me. To keep up my job skills, I took on an important consulting job for David Jeffrey's firm. This assignment required frequent travel to the client in Philadelphia, long hours crunching numbers and writing at home, and a tight deadline for my presentation to the client's board of directors. Child care was a great concern, because Patrick was six and Caroline only three. I couldn't find reliable baby-sitting help, my in-laws were busy with their own lives, and my parents were too old and too far away to help out. I worked nights and weekends when Pat could baby-sit. I was short on sleep and under a tremendous amount of stress.

I vividly remember the worst moment from this time of my life. I was standing in the checkout line at the Randall's supermarket near my home in Houston at nine-thirty on a Saturday night. I'd been working all day at my father-in-law's home office while Pat watched the children. On my way home, I'd stopped to pick up our weekly groceries. I was so exhausted I could have cried. And there in front of me was Diana's photograph on a magazine cover, again. I *really* wanted to live her life that night.

What I didn't know back then was that Diana was feeling equally desperate, but for very different reasons. I was feeling the commonplace stresses of time, money, and fatigue. Diana was suffering from loneliness and a sense of helplessness. She was trapped in an unhappy marriage and isolated within the royal family. Mine was the better deal.

Despite the lack of glamour in my daily life, I have always felt loved, respected, and needed by my husband and, of course, my children. For years, I did not realize that Diana longed for the simple companionship and freedom that ordinary people take for granted. Most of all, Diana needed a loving and supportive home life—someone to be there for her, always. This basic element of personal happiness seems so simple but can be so elusive. If that foundation is missing, all the glamour in the world can't make up for it, as Diana knew. In keeping with the positive and cheerful nature of our correspondence, neither of us wrote about our problems.

During this stressful period, Pat and I were cheered by an unexpected and brief encounter with royalty. In February 1986, Prince Charles was speaking at an elegant evening fund-raiser in Houston. Jack and Laura Lee Blanton, our good friends, very thoughtfully invited us to attend as their guests. Jack was then head of the Houston Chamber of Commerce, which was a sponsor of the event. In 1981, the Blantons had arranged for our chauffeured car in London for Diana's wedding and knew of our continuing friendship, including our recent visit in Washington.

Laura Lee was seated next to Sir Oliver Wight, the British ambassador, at dinner. Pat and I sat far across the large table for twelve. On our behalf, Laura Lee asked the ambassador if he thought Prince Charles might like to see us later. She opened the conversation by asking politely, "Do you remember the Robertsons, who are friends of the Princess of Wales?"

Ambassador Wight exclaimed, "I'll never forget the Robertsons!" He explained that the Princess of Wales had insisted that she have time to see Patrick and me during their Washington visit the previous fall. Her request had "wreaked havoc" on the embassy's schedule for the royal couple. Fortunately for Patrick and me, the Wights' gracious manners that afternoon had given no hint of their frustration with our visit. I can only imagine how displeased the embassy and royal staffs must have been when our visit went on for so long. How wonderful it had been of Diana to insist on seeing us. Ambassador Wight was good-natured as he recalled that day, so Laura Lee continued, "The Robertsons are here tonight. Do you think His Royal Highness would like to speak with them for a minute at the end of the evening?" The ambassador checked with Prince Charles. The answer was yes.

Pat and I listened attentively to Prince Charles's after-dinner speech, which covered trade relations. He was articulate and witty. His voice sounded marvelous, as always, with the slight gravelly undertone that gave it resonance.

After most of the guests had left the ballroom, Pat and I joined a line of perhaps two dozen people privileged to speak briefly with the guest of honor in a quiet corner in the lobby.

When Prince Charles approached us, he needed no visible prompting. Warm and natural, he greeted me: "Mrs. Robertson, how are you? And how is Patrick doing? Still playing soccer?" Pat bowed, while I curtsied and murmured, "Your Royal Highness."

I was pretty good at this routine by now. I replied that Patrick was happy and busy and that I hoped his sons were as well. I expressed our delight at seeing him again and my profound appreciation for our visit the previous fall. I reintroduced Pat to Prince Charles and reminded the prince that they'd met at the party before the wedding. Of course, I asked to be remembered to the Princess of Wales. Closing with, "A great pleasure to see you both, again," Prince Charles moved on, poised and unhurried. Once again, I was impressed by his elegant bearing and gracious presence—clearly born and trained to be a king. He has such great personal charm that I've never even noticed close up that his ears stick out. I truly like what I've seen of Prince Charles.

On the way home, I talked to Pat about the arduous nature of the royals' official duties. Prince Charles has to deliver countless focused and witty speeches, shake hundreds of hands, make dozens and dozens of polite com-

Diana has always been openly affectionate and tactile.
She was extraordinarily warm and tender with Patrick.
He adored his young nanny.

LEFT: One morning in September 1980, Diana told me there were reporters and photographers waiting in the mews outside our house. She'd spent the weekend at Balmoral with Prince Charles at the invitation of "his mother." Although the press followed Diana from that day on, she continued to look after Patrick throughout the courtship. (Photo © Photographers International)

BELOW: Diana was Patrick's nanny for most of 1980. She enthusiastically played with him, read to him, fed him lunch, and took him out for walks—busy, happy days for both of them. Diana clearly loved being with children.

RIGHT: Diana picked out this bright yellow jacket for Patrick in early spring. He wore the jacket on many of our travels throughout England and Scotland. Later that spring she gave him a yellow rubber bathtub duck as a present.

BELOW: Diana had told the nanny agency she would work only in S.W. 1, 3, or 7, the most central residential areas of London. How lucky for us that we lived in S.W. 1! In February 1980, Diana came for her interview at our flat in Belgrave Square.

ABOVE: In November 1985, Diana insisted on taking time out from a world tour to see Patrick and me in Washington. I was amazed that Prince Charles joined us for the lengthy private visit and that he was kind enough to talk for some time with Patrick.

OPPOSITE TOP: Here I am with my husband, Pat, all dressed up for the glamorous ball at Buckingham Palace two nights before the wedding. Diana greeted me with a huge hug in the receiving line and introduced us as "Patrick's parents" to her future husband, Prince Charles.

OPPOSITE BOTTOM: On the morning of the wedding, Pat and I posed in front of a friend's house in Brompton Square before we were driven to St. Paul's through the jubilant crowds lining the procession route. We were deeply touched that Diana had invited us to the "wedding of the century."

ABOVE: Diana greeted Patrick, Caroline, and me with enthusiastic hugs at a luncheon at her home in Kensington Palace in 1992. Before lunch we exchanged presents in her elegant formal drawing room. This is the same setting that Diana chose for her 1993 Christmas photo of herself with her sons.

OPPOSITE TOP: Diana suggested taking a picture outdoors in the Kensington Palace garden after the luncheon. Patrick and Caroline had just visited with Prince Harry in his room.

OPPOSITE BOTTOM: My husband, Pat, enjoyed his only private conversation with Diana when he came to pick us up after our luncheon. Her direct and unaffected manner made an unforgettable impression on him.

ABOVE LEFT: Around the trees outside Kensington Palace, mourners placed flowers, pictures, and messages, lit by countless flickering candles, creating dozens of "shrines" to their beloved princess.

ABOVE RIGHT: Here is where I gazed at the closed and darkened private gate to Kensington Palace where Diana's casket rested the night before her funeral. This is the same entrance my family and I had driven through to visit Diana on a sunny, summer day just a few years earlier.

BELOW: On Sunday afternoon, the day after Diana's funeral, people by the thousands continued to bring flowers and messages to Kensington Palace.

ments, smile constantly, travel thousands of miles, sleep in unfamiliar rooms. All this may look glamorous, but really it's hard work—a luxurious drill, but a drill, nonetheless.

Soon after this quick brush with royalty, our family crises were happily resolved. Pat's career with Exxon continued with a move back to New Jersey. My consulting job was wrapped up successfully with a solid presentation to the client's directors and the best written report I had ever produced.

We spent the summer of 1986 moving once again. This time, we chose Mountain Lakes, a small, old-fashioned community in central New Jersey where we already knew a few families from Exxon and The Morgan Bank. We lived there for four years—a record for us. As soon as we were settled, I wrote to Diana to give her our new address and family news.

Diana replied in late November after returning from a trip to the Middle East, which she had found "fascinating." Then she wrote, "I wish I could persuade you to come and visit us over here as I think a great deal of Patrick and I shall never forget that adorable face in Washington with the blue blazer, tie with pheasants on and a junior pair of shoes on that my husband had on at the time!" What a memory and what fondness to recall Patrick's outfit a year later!

Her boys were growing up, too. William would start nursery school in January of 1987 at four and a half. The most exciting part for William was the uniform, "which he is thrilled to bits about, especially as Harry is very envious of his big brother!" The next year would find Diana and Charles in Portugal, Spain, and Germany. "It never stops and it's certainly no holiday package tour!" How true. I'd seen that for myself in Washington.

I had been thrilled to catch a television documentary on the royal couple and had said so in my letter. Diana wrote, "An awful lot of money was raised for very worthy causes so that made the intrusion much more worthwhile!" This comment exemplified the conflict Diana faced between her desire for privacy and her desire to do good.

Shortly before Christmas that year, Patrick, now seven, came along with me to work at our church's annual Christmas bazaar. As he wandered around, he spotted a small hand-crafted necklace and earring set. He thought of Diana's recent letter and remembered our visit in Washington. As a result, he bought the little jewelry set with his saved-up allowance. We sent it to Diana for Christmas, accompanied by notes from Patrick and me.

Later the following January, 1987, Diana wrote to "Dearest Patrick," telling him she was "enormously touched to be thought of in this wonderful way." Then she drew a smiley face. "I will wear the necklace and earrings with great pride and they will be a constant reminder of my dear friend in America. This comes with a big thank you and a *huge* hug, and as always, *lots* of love from *Diana.*" Could one imagine a more precious letter? I just felt chills of emotion when I redis-covered it after her death.

Diana wrote to me at the same time. Now that the holidays were over, Diana had to return to her official duties—"It's just like going back to school!" Prince William loved his new school. Diana felt he was ready for "stimulation from a new area and boys his own age. . . ." She described taking William to school the first day "in front of 200 press men and quite frankly I could easily have dived into a box of Kleenex as he look incredibly grown-up—too sweet!"

Diana noticed that Patrick and Caroline looked very much alike in our 1987 Christmas photograph. "But my goodness how they grow or maybe it's the years taking off and leaving us mothers behind!" Diana was a young twenty-six when she wrote that observation. I wonder if she knew then that less than four years later, Prince William would be off to boarding school, truly leaving his mother behind. Again she extended a welcoming invitation. If we could manage a trip to London, "I'd love to introduce you to my two men!" By then, she meant her two sons. She also repeated that our letters "mean a great deal to me. . . ."

As I reread Diana's letters now, marveling at her kindness and mourning her loss, I cannot recall what last-minute calamities prevented my visiting Diana during the late 1980s. What could I have been thinking to miss these opportunities? I never doubted the sincerity of her feelings or her invitations. I know I was terrifically busy day to day with my children, part-time work, and household responsibilities, particularly with Pat traveling unpredictably and often. I believed that Diana was happily ensconced in her splendid royal life. The thought of my friendship with her provided a constant bright spot in my life.

I assumed that we would continue to write to each other and visit when we could over a long lifetime. I was not aware of her marital and health problems, or I would have flown over to offer whatever comfort or advice I could, as an older, maybe wiser, friend. I assumed the early press reports of trouble in her marriage were either gossip or exaggeration. When I read of the royal couple's month-long separation in the fall of 1987, I thought of my husband's frequent month-long business trips and did not consider it unusual. I didn't realize that her life was unraveling inexorably. If only she'd written that she needed to talk or wanted advice. True to her private and discreet nature, she never wrote a single word about her troubles. I only learned the true state of affairs years later from the press.

During the summer of 1989, a banker acquaintance, Don Roberts, who was a senior vice-president at U.S. Trust, called to tell me that he and his wife would be attending an exclusive fund-raiser at Highgrove in early August. Mr. Roberts knew of our connection with Diana because I had been consulting at U.S. Trust during the summer of 1981 and needed a week off to attend the royal wedding. The purpose of his recent call was to ask if I would like to send along a letter or anything else that he could deliver personally to Diana at the luncheon fund-raiser. I carefully composed a letter to Diana, which I mailed to Mr. Roberts for hand delivery to Diana. With my letter, I sent Mr. Roberts my copy of Penny Junor's biography of Prince Charles as background reading for his trip.

As soon as Mr. Roberts returned, he called to give me a full report. He said he was amazed and that I would have been touched by Diana's spontaneous reaction. He was introduced to Her Royal Highness in the receiving line. After bowing and greeting her, he pulled my letter out of his inside pocket and said, "I've brought you a letter from Mrs. Robertson." She didn't hesitate for an instant, exclaiming, "How wonderful! How is she and how is Patrick?" Instant recognition, although we hadn't seen each other for four years.

A few days later Diana wrote to me. She mentioned how Mr. Roberts had "cheered the occasion up by producing one letter! How marvelous to hear about Patrick. . . ." Then, "I have been searching for a prep school for next year and it's an awful thought that William will be away from home—An English habit I'm afraid!" I understood Diana's reluctance to give up her son at eight years old.

I remembered the many English youngsters home from boarding school with whom I'd talked in our Belgrave Square garden back in 1980. Without exception, they felt unhappy at being sent away from home. I felt sorry that Diana had not been able to keep William at home for longer, but I doubt that she had a choice. The English upper classes almost always send their children away to school, and at a young age. At least Diana had managed to send her sons to a private day school in their early years rather than the isolating at-home tutoring Prince Charles and his royal siblings had experienced.

I could never have given up my children at eight, as Diana did. I didn't even consider boarding school for Patrick or Caroline at the standard American age of fourteen or fifteen. I loved the daily contact of car pools and ball games, homework and field trips, family dinners and bedtime stories. Now that Patrick has left for college, I definitely know that I made the right decision for me. If Diana had been free to decide, I wonder what her choice would have been.

In November 1989, Pat accepted a three-year assignment in Jakarta, Indonesia. He left for Asia in late January 1990. I waited the five months until June to allow Patrick and Caroline to finish the school year, to sell our house, to tidy up financial and legal loose ends, and, of course, to pack up our increasingly full house. Once again, I was coping with the unvarying pattern of corporate moves on my own.

One unexpected problem with moving to developing countries is that their postal systems don't work. I was also surprised to find that Exxon had no mail-forwarding system for its several hundred expatriates. I was lucky to find Candi Healion, a good-hearted secretary, to forward our essential mail once a week via the company's internal courier system. Critical mail meant credit card bills, financial records, and personal correspondence—most importantly, Diana's Christmas cards and any letters. In May, I had, as usual, written to Diana to give her our new forwarding address. Thanks to Candi, we received her Christmas cards every year.

I was a poor correspondent that first year in Jakarta. I was desperately ill for the first six months with tropical sprue, a form of anemia, and a virulent tummy bug I couldn't shake. Just learning the language and trying to get some semblance of order in our lives, especially the children's, took all my energy. I had very little cheerful to write about for a long time. I hasten to say that the brightest spot in a difficult year was the Indonesian people, who were friendly and welcoming.

I felt frustrated that I couldn't send letters to Diana as I normally had via reliable U.S. certified mail. I never thought of fax machines or international courier services. Regrettably, I let my relationship with Diana lapse for a time in 1990 and 1991.

We heard and read very little about the Princess of Wales during that time. There were no English-language news shows and very few English-language magazines and newspapers. We did receive a slimmed-down version of *Time* magazine. News of her personal problems had begun to trickle out in the press by this time. Our expatriate friends would tell us if they had read or heard news about Diana when they traveled. One English couple, in particular, the Lavings from British Petroleum, were quite current on the news from London. From these varied and sporadic sources, we realized that Diana's "fairy tale" had never been true. We learned, for instance, that Diana had refused her husband's offer of a thirtieth birthday party for her and that Prince Charles was seriously involved with another woman. I was totally surprised and very sorry for Diana. She was such a decent and good person; she deserved much better. Unfortunately, I still hadn't figured out how to send mail from Indonesia to England.

By the spring of 1992, I'd adjusted quite well to life in Jakarta. I'd made some wonderful friends and had become actively involved at the children's school. By March, I was busy planning our family's summer vacation. We'd decided to revisit England that year . We had many happy memories from 1980. Now I *had* to find a way to communicate with Diana. I was worried about her and wanted to see how she was for myself.

∽

*P*at and I finally realized we could use our friends at Exxon's office in London to send a letter to Diana. On March 18th, I wrote to Diana explaining my long silence and telling her the three-week period during which we would be in the vicinity of London. I asked if we might arrange a brief visit with her. A friend at Exxon's London office said he would be glad to have my letter delivered. His secretary, Nicky Collins, called the switchboard at Buckingham Palace to reach the Office of the Princess of Wales at St. James's Palace. Nicky explained our connection with the Princess to one of Diana's secretaries, who instructed her to mail our letter to her attention at St. James's Palace to be dealt with there. She gave no assurance that it would be sent on to Diana at Kensington Palace. Personal mail for Diana did not seem to be very welcome. This carefully guarded and roundabout route appeared to have several locations at which Diana's mail could be stopped, delayed, or screened. In fact, I've often wondered if my later letters ever reached Diana. Early that spring, we did not yet know the full extent of Diana's troubles with her marriage and the royal family. After waiting for two months, I'd given up expecting a reply.

Happily, on May 20 we received a fax at Pat's office in Jakarta from Patrick Jephson, Diana's private secretary at that time, saying, "It is hoped that Thursday 25th June might be a convenient date for lunch." The invitation was extended to our entire family. We faxed a reply immediately. Once again, I was stunned by Diana's kindness. I'd hoped for a quick hello and hug on the front steps of Kensington Palace, not lunch for the entire family in her home. I thought, "God bless her. She's pulled through for us again. What an angel!" The June 25 date was lucky, too. That week we would still be within driving distance of London, at a charming rental cottage in the Cotswolds. On Saturday the 27th we were driving on to Wales. I was thrilled at the prospect of having a real visit with Diana again.

Our departure for London in early June was delayed because I became ill and was bedridden in Jakarta for more than a week. By the time the children and I met Pat in London, I was still feeling dreadful. I'd lost at least ten pounds, so I felt weak and looked haggard. After an eighteen-hour trip, I was suffering from jet lag and insomnia. I was certainly not going to be at my best when we saw Diana.

I called Diana's office at Saint James's Palace as soon as we were settled in our cozy rental flat in Kensington to confirm the lunch date and to leave telephone numbers where her office could reach us. The *Sunday Times* had just begun to excerpt sections of Andrew Morton's first book, *Diana: Her True Story*. The book caused a sensation. For the first time, Pat and I read all about the breakdown of Diana's marriage, her long-running unhappiness, and her bulimia. We were appalled by the extent of her problems. Pat and I concealed the newspaper articles from Patrick, who was a great reader, and only told the children that Diana had been unhappy in her marriage. We worried that Diana would feel so pressured by the publicity surrounding the book that her office might call off our lunch. And now, of course, I wanted to see her more than ever. I needed to be assured by her that she was all right. I worried every time the telephone rang in the London flat, then later in our rented house in the Cotswolds, that our meeting would be canceled. It never occurred to me that Diana would find a relaxing lunch with old friends a welcome antidote to the uproar over the revelations in the book.

Caroline, now nine, was eager to meet the Princess of Wales, who had become her ideal of beauty and grace. Her favorite book for years had been *Royal Style Wars*, which consisted of hundreds of color photographs by Tim Graham of Diana and the Duchess of York. Caroline and her friends in Jakarta loved to pore over the color pages to compare Diana's fashion sense to Fergie's. Diana always won out in their biased judgment. Caroline wanted to see her dream princess in person. She was terribly envious that her brother had been the baby lucky enough to have a fairy-tale nanny.

Caroline and I had our own fashion crisis before the lunch. We'd been unable to find dress shoes for Caroline in Jakarta. I had been feeling so shaky as I packed after my illness that I'd packed the wrong shoes for myself. Caroline and I spent an afternoon at Harrod's, where we found the only pair of dressy shoes they had in her size—a very sweet pair of silvery ballerina flats. Not quite right for lunchtime, but they would have to do. I found a classic low-heeled Ferragamo pump for myself that cost 50 percent more than the same shoes would have cost in New York due to the exchange rate. I've worn my shoes constantly ever since. I think of Diana and that lunch every time I slip them on.

The week of our scheduled lunch, we were staying outside London in Chipping Camden, a picture-book village in the Cotswolds. Patrick and Caroline had both caught colds from running around in the large garden with bare feet late in the day. They were so happy to play in cool, clear summer weather after the humidity and pollution in Jakarta. They were both sniffling and wheezing as Thursday the

25th approached. I was still feeling dreadful—tired and depressed. Pat tried to cheer me up by saying, "You'll be all right. You're just nervous about seeing Diana." I was frustrated by his simple solution to a complex problem—an illness and depression that were not going away. I snapped back at him, "That's not the problem. I've *never* been nervous about seeing Diana." The royal trappings around Diana may have been intimidating, but Diana as a person had always been warm and unaffected.

Pat did not want to drive into London and cope with the traffic. I refused to take the train and risk arriving rumpled at Kensington Palace. I was still feeling very weak and needed the ease and comfort of door-to-door transportation. Pat finally agreed. He could tell I was in bad shape, but I managed to pull myself together for our eagerly awaited visit. That Thursday morning, a beautiful, sunny day, we all woke up early to prepare for the two-hour drive into London. Pat and Patrick wore navy blazers, button-down oxford-cloth shirts with ties, and slacks. Caroline had on a simple cotton flowered dress that we'd ordered from a dressmaker in Jakarta because we couldn't find anything appropriate in the few stores there. I wore a soft red, green, and cream jacket made from native Indonesian fabric and beige silk slacks. Nothing too dressy for a daytime appointment.

While we were still in our flat in London, I had checked the local street map and walked over to the motor entrance to Kensington Palace so we'd know where to go on the 25th.

The gated driveway was just off Kensington Road at the western edge of Kensington Gardens. That Thursday, when we arrived at the entrance gate, Pat looked at the "Private Road" sign and refused to drive up that road. He insisted on driving around the neighborhood to find a public-access road and, of course, couldn't find one. Then he spotted a London policeman and asked him for directions.

The bobby directed us to the "Private Road" we'd already passed, but added, "You won't be able to drive up there. It's restricted."

Pat nudged me, so I said, "Oh, it's all right, Officer. We have an appointment with the Princess of Wales."

The policeman shook his head in disbelief and said, "Right-o. Sure you do. Good day."

We drove right back to where we had started and proceeded through an open gateway framed by two square brick columns, both marked "Private Road."

Just before we reached the gravel courtyard next to the palace, we came to a small guardhouse. I told the two guards who we were and explained, "We've been invited to lunch with Her Royal Highness."

They laughed, "Which one?"

I blushed at my mistake. "The Princess of Wales," I specified. I had forgotten that Their Royal Highnesses, Princess Margaret and Princess Michael of Kent, as well as the Duchess of Gloucester, also had apartments at Kensington Palace.

The guards politely directed Pat to a parking place near the courtyard. Pat chose not to join us for lunch because he did not want to impose on my realtionship with Diana.

Patrick, Caroline, and I were directed toward Diana's front door, where a quiet, gracious man, whom I took to be her butler, welcomed us into a cool, dark ground-floor entrance hall. The hallway was dimly lit from its one window and the front door. A single flight of stairs to Diana's apartment rose along one side of the hall, and doorways to what I assumed were offices or service rooms led off another side. This entrance appeared to lead only to Diana's quarters. To our left, as we entered, were powder rooms where we could freshen up. The one Caroline and I used was decorated with flowered wallpaper, a mirror over the basin, standard fixtures, and linen towels—very much like my own powder room.

The butler led us up a gray stone stairway into an elegant formal drawing room. Diana had not yet returned from a soccer game at William's school, which was an hour away from London. The drawing room was quite large, forty or fifty feet square, with large traditional double-hung windows along one wall. The room held several seating groups with sofas, chairs, and tables in predominantly eighteenth-century French style. The colors were warm and pale, apricots and yellows, and the fabrics were elegant, silks and brocades that shone softly in the midday sunlight. The feeling was one of understated, but undeniable, luxury. The many beautifully framed photographs placed on tabletops and on the piano caught my eye. My favorites were the beautiful silver-framed black-and-white photographs of Diana with her sons by Patrick de Marchelier.

Diana's butler offered us cool drinks while we waited for a few minutes. Patrick and Caroline sat on a yellow brocade sofa beneath a large antique tapestry. Our presents for Diana and her boys lay on the table in front of them. The following year, Diana's Christmas card had a picture of her with her sons posed behind that same sofa in front of the tapestry. I sat in a Louis XV armchair facing the doorway. We were quite relaxed because this time we were seeing only Diana, our beloved friend and correspondent, in her own home. Then the door from the hallway opened suddenly.

Diana burst into the room—radiant, beaming, exuberant—like a graceful, long-legged colt. Her enthusiasm and energy struck us instantly. She was clearly having a good day. It made *us* feel good just to be in the same room.

At thirty-one, Diana seemed all grown up and very much her own person. She appeared freer in her actions and noticeably more confident and spontaneous than when I had last seen her in 1985. Now, she was thriving successfully on her own, no longer deferring to her husband.

Her cheeks and nose were slightly sunburned from her morning outdoors. She seemed to have on little or no makeup and she wore only a watch and a small ring. She looked fresh and natural. I noticed that she no longer bit her fingernails, a very good sign. She wore a white tailored jacket over a bright turquoise dress printed with red, pink, and white flowers, low heels, and bare legs. She was a breath of fresh air.

I stood up as she almost flew across the floor with her arms outstretched. I wasn't quite sure what I should do and gulped, "Umm, shouldn't I curtsy . . . or something first?" Diana replied, "Absolutely not. I *loathe* formality!" We gave each other a big hug. Then she scooted around the coffee table to hug Patrick and Caroline, who were on their feet by now, following my example.

Diana sat down on the sofa next to my children as we began our visit. This was an irresistible "photo op," so I asked Diana's permission and snapped a picture. Diana apologized for being late. She had taken Prince Harry from school for the day so he could join her at his big brother's soccer game. She often visited William at his sports games.

She quickly asked us a series of questions about all of us. Where were we staying? Had we recovered from our jet lag? What had we seen in London? What had the children particularly enjoyed? She kept smiling at my children. She was positively effervescent. Patrick was very polite, but rather quiet, a bit self-conscious at thirteen. Caroline, totally entranced, beamed up at Diana. At nine, Caroline was still too young to feel awkward.

Diana asked if I was still working, because "I remember how important your career was to you." She had recalled our discussion in 1980 about my staying home to raise Patrick. *I'd* forgotten how important my career had once seemed to me—it had been so long ago—but Diana remembered from twelve years earlier.

Next we exchanged presents. Diana gave us a dark blue leather photo album, for my travel pictures again. We'd brought handmade presents from Indonesia, souvenirs from the exotic part of the world where we now lived. For her boys, we'd chosen handcarved, brightly painted wooden animals from Bali. For Diana, I'd selected, with the help of a fashion-savvy friend, a simple gray silk jacket with a striking blue and gold pattern. We thought the jacket would look dramatic over black pants or a simple black dress—we both owned similar jackets. Diana was clearly startled by the jacket. It was too exotic for her taste. I could tell she didn't like it at all, but quickly hid her dismay with a smile and a tactful remark like, "How very colorful," or "How very useful." It was quite funny. I hastened to explain that the jacket was meant as a souvenir, not as a serious fashion item.

At this point lunch was announced and we moved next door into a simply furnished dining room decorated in peach and apricot shades. The sideboards and chairs were in formal English styles, Sheridan or Hepplewhite, as I recall. The four of us sat at a round table. Patrick was on Diana's left, Caroline on her right. I sat facing Diana with my back to the windows. This was fortunate, since I felt a million years old as I looked across at Diana's youth and vitality. A fresh flower arrangement filled the center of the table, which was set with pale table linens, elegant bone china, and beautiful old silver. A traditional, pretty lunch setting.

The menu and service were quite sophisticated. Diana's butler hovered unobtrusively in the background, while a footman wearing gray suede gloves passed the various courses on silver serving trays. Diana asked if I'd like a glass of white wine. I declined and we both drank iced tea. The lunch menu consisted of a seafood appetizer, creamy chicken in a pastry shell, and a green salad—none of which was really kids' food. Patrick and Caroline toyed silently with their seafood and managed a few obligatory bites. I noticed Diana's eyes twinkling with amusement as she watched them. I had to admit, "Patrick and Caroline aren't especially fond of shellfish." When the chicken was served, Caroline didn't know how to serve herself and cast an imploring look at me that said, "Oh, help! What do I do, Mom?"

Before I could react, Diana, so attuned to children, jumped up and came over to serve Caroline and cut up her chicken. I was speechless at her rapid, sympathetic response. Caroline thanked her, then gazed at her in adoration for the rest of the meal. She was in heaven! Dessert was tricky and delicious—ice cream in a slippery chocolate shell. This time two people served all of us, so my children would not have to struggle for themselves.

During lunch, Diana made a point of asking Patrick and Caroline about their travels, their schools, and their hobbies. Patrick's responses were very polite, but tended to be rather subdued and brief. I wanted him to sound a bit more animated. I resisted the urge to give him a sharp kick under the table. Caroline was more talkative. Diana seemed to enjoy my lively, spunky daughter.

My children behaved themselves beautifully amidst the unaccustomed formality and luxury. My years of daily training paid off. They answered questions politely, sat up straight in their chairs, and even chewed with their mouths closed. I thought of my mother-in-law's claim, "You can take those children anywhere." Their lunch with the Princess of Wales certainly proved her point. I was very proud of them.

Throughout the lunch, at least one of Diana's domestic staff was present, as were my children. This was a personal, but a not a private, meeting. I never mentioned the just-published Andrew Morton book, her marriage, or her husband. There was tremendous speculation about the extent of Diana's cooperation in the book. If she had talked, she obviously wanted her side of the story known. As Diana and I conversed across the table, she expressed her views in a forthright manner that showed how confident and independent she had become.

Diana had opened the lunch conversation by asking with a mischievous grin, "How are you enjoying living in Jakarta?"

I confessed that the climate, pollution, and congestion took some getting used to, but that the Indonesian people were welcoming and helpful and that made up for a lot.

She smiled and said, "I'd wondered how you were getting along there." She and her husband had paid a state visit to Indonesia in the late 1980s. She agreed that the heat and humidity were hard to bear. She laughed as she told us, "We just seemed to go to a lot of formal banquets all over the place. Is there anything else to do there?"

I explained that seeing the local culture often involved inconvenient travel to remote or primitive locations, so two or three days would not have been adequate time. In fact, I'd been too sick or too busy with my family to see much myself. I was surprised by what a humorous and outspoken traveler Diana had become. She would never have been so direct when I saw her in 1985.

I raised the very general topic of relations with the royal family, based on what I'd been reading in the English newspapers since I'd arrived. Diana said that the widely held belief that the Queen Mother had guided her during the period of her engagement was "completely untrue." She'd received virtually no support or advice from the royal family, ever. I laughed when Diana good-naturedly referred to the royal family as "that lot." She went on, "They never praise you when you do something right, but they certainly let you know when you've done something wrong."

Diana proceeded to say that she had "little use for the

upper classes." This comment intrigued me, since she'd been born and raised among the aristocracy. Her attitude marked a true departure from her past. Diana found "ordinary people so much more real." She loved her contact with people and related two incidents as examples.

She had recently been driving her own car in London and had stopped for a traffic light. A total stranger recognized her, walked over, and immediately told her how worried he was about his wife's illness. Diana was sympathetic to his anxiety and touched by his need. To me, this story demonstrated how sincerely her compassion for others came across. A complete stranger felt comfortable speaking to her about his deepest worry and she responded with natural concern.

Then she told us about going to Harrod's to buy a video game that Prince William particularly wanted for his birthday. She confessed that she "felt a perfect fool," since she didn't know how video games worked or exactly which item William wanted. I could relate to that. The video-game craze was too technical for me, too. As she walked through Harrod's, the other shoppers cleared way for her. They did not stop her or intrude. They only wanted to smile at her, say "hello," or simply gaze at her in person. Diana's point was that she loved the genuine friendliness and politeness of the people she encountered. Clearly, Diana needed the reassurance of the sincere support of "ordinary people," or she would not have ventured to shops, restaurants, and amusement parks as she did. She could so easily have remained behind the palace walls, aloof and isolated.

Turning to Patrick and Caroline, Diana asked if I had trouble getting them to do their homework. They both replied, "No, we just sit down and do it." I know I embarrassed Patrick when I told Diana what a good student he was turning out to be. With a grin, Diana confessed, "I have to bribe my boys to do their homework." The bribes were only little treats, like a piece of candy.

Diana was determined to teach her sons about the real world and how people live. She was trying to give Prince William, at ten, and Prince Harry, soon to turn eight, as "normal an upbringing as possible," given their station in life. With regard to this aim, she observed, "My husband thinks I'm overdoing it." This was her only reference to Prince Charles that afternoon. For instance, so that the boys would learn to handle money, Diana gave them pocket money to buy candy and other small treats in the local shops in Tetbury, the market town near Highgrove, the royal couple's country estate.

It had been difficult to send William to boarding school at eight, but it was not as harsh as it sounded, Diana assured me. Parents could visit on weekends and come to watch sports matches, as she and Harry had done that morning. Also, the boys were allowed to come home for a weekend about once a month. Harry would be joining his big brother at Ludgrove in September.

"After prep school," I asked, "where will you send Prince William? Not to Gordonstoun, I hope." Gordonstoun was the boarding school in northern Scotland where Prince Charles had been unhappy as a teenager.

"Oh, no," Diana answered. "I'd like William to go to Eton, if he can get in."

I smiled, "I don't imagine that will be a problem."

Prince William is currently attending Eton and Prince Harry is finishing up at Ludgrove.

As Diana talked openly with my children and me, she made the statement that has defined her forever in my mind:

"My boys mean everything to me. They're my life."

I looked directly across the table at her, gestured toward Patrick and Caroline with my hands outstretched toward them, and replied, "I know exactly how you feel." It was a wonderful moment, sharing our common devotion to our children.

I mentioned to Diana that she seemed to be attracting more press attention as time went on. She replied, "I never read anything about myself in the press. I find it too upsetting." I took her to mean that she found the unkind, untrue, or critical pieces too hurtful and she'd rather not know. I didn't blame her. I assumed that her staff kept track of her media exposure. It would have been a full-time job.

We then touched upon her fashion image. She seemed baffled by all the "fuss" about her clothes because "It's not what I'm about, at all." Clearly Diana enjoyed making an impact with her good looks and smashing wardrobe. Who wouldn't? She was a born beauty who always looked terrific with seemingly little effort. If she ever took a bad picture, I never saw it. I had the impression that she viewed this aspect of her life as fun, not to be taken very seriously.

Appearances at fund-raisers, arts performances, concerts, and movie openings were part of Diana's public life. She enjoyed meeting new people, often other celebrities, at these galas. She specifically mentioned how much she had enjoyed meeting Liza Minnelli at a benefit a few months earlier. Her main problem with these evening events was the late hours. She said she had "trouble staying up past midnight." Her idea of a good time was to curl up with her boys for the evening and read or watch a movie and get to sleep early. I thought of Prince Harry turning eight and going off to prep school in September. I wondered how Diana would fill her free evenings then, if she wasn't really a party person? What a shame she never had the dozen children she had wished for at nineteen.

At this point, Prince Harry entered the dining room. He was an enchanting child, with finely chiseled features and the Spencer coloring—soft red hair and light freckles. He was polite and poised, with a happy, mischievous smile. He was dressed rather formally in a jacket, tie, and slacks, like Patrick. If I'd known him well enough, I'd have given him a hug—he was so appealing. Diana explained that Harry had eaten his lunch with his nanny in the kitchen and was now ready to meet his mother's guests. He stood by the table between Caroline and me as Diana introduced the three of us to her younger son. We did not bow or call him "Your Royal Highness," since this was an informal gathering. Besides, Prince Harry was only seven. Diana had noticed Caroline getting restless, squirming a bit in her chair, and empathized. "I know. It's so hard to sit still. Harry, would you like to show Patrick and Caroline your room?" Off the three children went, but Diana's butler remained to serve coffee.

Now that Diana and I were more or less alone, I could express my deep concern for her. "The London papers have been full of excerpts from that new book. What an awful lot you've been through! I didn't really know before. I've been so worried about you. Are you going to be all right?"

Diana admitted she'd had a very rough time. She was too discreet to mention any specifics and must have realized that I knew the basic facts from the newspapers. She hastened to add, "But I'm fine now. I know what I have to do." Her first priority was to raise her boys. Then, she was seeking a new path for her life now that her sons were growing up and her marriage was over. She expressed her deep and genuine commitment to helping people who were sick and lonely and neglected. She wanted to use her position and energy to work for good causes. She mentioned her tremendous admiration for Mother Teresa, as a truly good, selfless person. Diana did not specify which causes or charities she had in mind. I believe she was just beginning to see herself as a working humanitarian and had not yet narrowed down the causes she could most effectively serve. At this time, June of 1992, I assumed that she would find her own way but still remain loosely within the structure of the royal family—a difficult balancing act. I wonder if Diana knew then that she would be officially separated from Prince Charles before year's end.

Since it was clear she would not receive any support from her husband or his family, I asked her to whom she would turn for guidance. She felt very lucky to have good friends who gave her advice when she asked for it and who also "let me know when I'm about to make a wrong step." She didn't mention her friends by name and I didn't ask.

The excerpts from the Morton book had mentioned several close personal friends. I assumed Diana was referring to some of them. I found it surprising and rather sad that she did not mention any members of her family as a source of support and advice. Diana had seemed to be close to her sister Lady Jane and her brother, Charles, in 1980. She'd taken Patrick to play with her sister's daughter and had asked for time off to see her brother when he came to London. But, of course, that was long ago and so much had changed.

I apologized for being such a poor correspondent from Jakarta and promised to do better. She assured me that she still received her personal mail and opened it herself. I wasn't so sure, given the long delay with my letter in March. She said she would look forward to my letters in the future. Sometime later, I read reports in the press that Diana's mail was, in fact, being screened.

Then I cleared my throat and said cautiously, "You've been so kind to see us today. I don't want to be a nuisance, but would it be all right if I also wrote the next time we plan to come to England? I don't imagine we'd get here more than every eight to ten years. But I would so love to see you again, if it's at all possible."

Diana smiled reassuringly and said she'd be happy to see us whenever we came to London. At that time, I still thought she'd be the Queen one day and eventually become too important to see us.

Diana's butler then announced that my husband was waiting in the drawing room. Our talk was coming to an end. I quickly asked her one more time, "Are you *sure* you're going to be all right?"

"Yes, Mrs. Robertson," Diana assured me. "Absolutely. You don't have to worry about me." She rose and walked next door to look after Pat, while I lingered over my coffee and thought about our conversation for a few moments.

I could hardly believe the remarkable transformation I'd seen that day. This was definitely a brand-new Diana, all grown up and on her own. She seemed so mature, confident, and sensible after all she'd been through. I thought,

"She's really got her head screwed on right. Thank God."

Diana had spoken in a calm, matter-of-fact voice with wry good humor, often with a twinkle in her eye. Occasionally I heard a hint of ruefulness, a slight, "I should have known better" tone in her voice, though I never heard even a trace of criticism, complaint, or self-pity in her remarks.

Besides her new maturity and independence, the other big change I observed in Diana was her terrific sense of humor. I'd seen occasional flashes of it in her letters over the years, but it was evident now in her conversation. I couldn't recall noticing this in 1980, or even in 1985. She'd been shyer and more reserved back then.

In 1985, I'd been spellbound by her dazzling outer beauty and poise. I could see that a more experienced and confident inner person was emerging gradually. By 1992, the inner Diana had been transformed by her personal struggles beyond anything I could have foreseen in 1980. She still possessed the qualities I had always loved—kindness, compassion, and a lack of pretension. She had since developed self-confidence, focus, and strength.

In the meantime, Pat was enjoying his first solo conversation with Diana. Previously, he'd seen her only twice at our flat in London in 1980 and again at the prewedding ball in 1981. Pat had been waiting on the palace driveway by our car. Diana's butler had come out and asked, "Are you Mr. Robertson?" Then he graciously said, "Please come inside." Pat expected to be shown into the entrance hall to wait more comfortably. He was pleasantly surprised to be led upstairs into Diana's elegant drawing room. There, Diana's butler gave him coffee and the newspaper to read while Diana and I finished our tête-à-tête.

Pat was caught unawares when Diana breezed in to see him. Pat is six feet three inches tall, but he was struck by Diana's height and by her natural good looks and vitality. He stood up, saying "Gosh, I don't know what to call you." Diana, unassuming and direct as always, replied, "Diana's just fine." They sat down together and had a short visit. Pat recalls that they talked about children, hers and ours, and our travel plans for Wales and Scotland. He couldn't get over how unaffected and natural she was. He was thrilled finally to visit with the wonderful Diana I'd been talking about for years.

Pat asked if we'd taken any photographs yet. Diana said, "Yes, but would you like to take another one outside in the garden?" I had finished my coffee and the children had returned from their tour, so we all walked downstairs and out onto the front courtyard and lawn. With my camera, Pat took a picture of Diana standing with the children and me. Then Diana asked one of her staff, who was standing nearby, to use my camera so that Pat could be in a photograph. Then with hugs and good wishes all around, we returned to our car and drove slowly from Kensington Palace. I hated to leave Diana, not knowing when, or even if, we'd see her again.

We were barely out of earshot when Caroline exclaimed, "Mummy, she's so beautiful and so nice. She's just perfect. What a jerk Charles must be!"

Pat and I burst out laughing at Caroline's blunt and irreverent assessment. Then we asked about the children's visit with Prince Harry.

Caroline reported first. "It didn't look like a prince's room at all, Mom. It looked just like ours. You know, full of books and toys and stuffed animals." I reminded Caroline that Diana wanted her boys to have a normal upbringing.

The only bit of conversation either of them could recall was Harry asking them quite seriously, "Do you two ever fight with each other?" Patrick and Caroline had laughed and said they certainly did. Harry seemed greatly relieved. "Good," he said, "because my brother and I fight all the time."

I couldn't coax any more details out of them.

We had enjoyed a wonderful, really unforgettable afternoon with Diana. I had been relieved to see her confident, healthy, and realistic—ready to move on to the next stage of her life. She had made an indelible and stunning impression on all of us. Pat and Caroline will certainly never forget their only close contact with the radiant and lovely Princess of Wales. Patrick adored seeing his princess again.

On balance, I felt quite optimistic about Diana's future that afternoon. Surely the worst was over for her. Nevertheless, a nagging doubt stuck in the back of my mind.

Diana had had a happy day with her boys and us, but I knew from the British papers that she'd endured many, many unhappy days during the past eleven years. Now that her marriage was acknowledged to be over and her second son was leaving for boarding school, I worried that she would be vulnerable to more lonely, low days. It could take a long time for her to recover from her disappointments and to refocus on her humanitarian causes. I fervently hoped that Diana would be all right from now on, but I felt a lingering concern.

∞

C H A P T E R

12

*A*fter our lunch with Diana, we continued our tour of Great Britain, then returned to America to see family and friends. As soon as it was available, I read the Andrew Morton book from cover to cover. For me, the book rang true, based on my own experience with Diana. Some part of what Morton had written I had heard directly from Diana at lunch the month before. In addition, the book contained the photograph of Diana holding Patrick I had taken and mailed to her before her wedding in 1981. No one else had a copy. Both Diana and the author denied having spoken directly to each other. Still, it seemed to me that Diana must have been aware of the contents of the book and had tacitly supported the friends who were cited as sources. I was glad that she had such loyal friends to speak out on her behalf.

My heart bled for Diana as I read about her years of disappointment and betrayal. It seemed she had never even been given a chance in her marriage. I have close friends who were dismayed to discover that their marriages were loveless. I could imagine from their experiences what Diana must have been through. Even worse, Diana had to face her troubles in the glare of publicity. At least that unhappy phase of her life was over. She had the devotion of her sons, the support of her friends, and the love and admiration of millions as a foundation for her new life.

Later that summer, while visiting Pat's parents in Houston, I discovered my fatigue was a result of a life-threatening blood disorder. My overwhelming fear was the possiblity of dying and leaving my children motherless.

A wonderful team of doctors quickly diagnosed and cured me. Still, I felt very vulnerable about returning to Jakarta where medical care was not dependable.

With our travel, my illness, and my depression, I had not managed to write a thank-you letter to Diana. I felt guilty about my thoughtlessness, but I just couldn't pull myself together to write that fall. By now, I was fully aware of Diana's tenuous personal situation. I couldn't imagine how she would carry on her public duties on days when she might be feeling depressed. At least I could stay home in privacy when I was having a bad day.

By year-end 1992, the news of Diana's separation had reached even Jakarta. I could imagine how difficult the decision to separate must have been for everyone concerned. I respected Diana's integrity in refusing to follow the outdated and hypocritical rules of marriages of convenience. I hoped she was managing to find her own way as she'd planned. I thought with irony about our respective situations. For a dozen years, I had thought Diana's life idyllic. Now, I wouldn't have traded places with her for anything in the world. I was grateful for the security and warmth of my family life.

In early December of 1992, Diana had sent a sepia-toned Christmas photograph of her boys only. This was the first time the entire family had not been portrayed in their annual card. Her sons were posed, Prince William seated and Prince Harry standing beside a ladder-backed chair against a bare background. The effect was wistful and somber. Diana's card had been mailed before the royal separation was announced, but the choice of subject and tone told me that something sad was coming.

After the 1992 Christmas holidays, I sent a letter to Diana by way of our friends at Exxon's London office again. I explained that I hadn't written sooner because I'd been seriously ill all summer and fall. I wrote of my fear of dying and leaving my children. I told her that I imagined her separation must have been painful, but it also must be a huge relief not to have to deal with an ambivalant situation any longer. I assured her of our continuing affection and support. For the first time, Diana did not write back. I assumed that she had never received my letter or was too upset about her own problems to write. I certainly knew that feeling.

During the summer of 1993, Patrick, Caroline, and I moved back to New Jersey without Pat. The Jakarta International School had proven to be hopelessly inadequate for both of them. Patrick was entering high school and needed the right preparation for college. Although we didn't know it that summer, Pat would not be home permanently for almost two years, and I became a single parent for that time. It was a real struggle. I spent hours every day driving my children to their separate schools and activities. I bought raw land and built a brand-new house in less than six months. I drove a five-hundred-mile round-trip to Vermont every month to help my parents during my father's final illness. And I tried to maintain friends and interests of my own. Some nights, as I talked to Pat on the phone, my body would shake from fatigue and stress. I wondered how in the world long-term single parents managed to keep going. This was a very unsettling two years for our family.

Back in America, it was easier to keep track of Diana in the news magazines. It seemed we were both struggling to rebuild our lives, under very different conditions. After her separation, Diana's life seemed to launch into high gear. I felt that she needed her good works and her social life to fill the void left with both her sons away at school. Every mother facing an empty nest needs a new focus. And Diana did not have the consolation of a solid marriage.

I followed Diana in the press and admired her from a distance again. I loved to see the press photos of her holding sick children, touching AIDS victims, bending down to speak to elderly hospital patients. I could imagine how much her warm and luminous presence would comfort them. This was the Diana I recognized—gentle, compassionate, and genuine. The Diana who'd cuddled my child for a year, who'd written tenderly to Nanny Chapman dying of cancer, who'd greeted me and my children with open arms. The glamorous celebrity was an increasingly important role for her, but I never felt it was the real Diana. Nonetheless, I marveled at her intelligence in using her fame and the everpresent media to highlight her favorite causes. I saw the public images of the grown-up Diana—beautiful, poised, and sophisticated. And I remembered the young Diana—gentle, shy, and unassuming. I wondered how the inner, private Diana was faring.

I was distressed that some of the press coverage of Diana was negative and critical. She was sometimes portrayed as high-strung and temperamental, even unstable. I couldn't reconcile these images with the Diana I had known. She had seemed so even-tempered and accommodating as a young woman. I found it impossible to believe that the events of the past several years could have changed her that much, but I had no up-to-date, firsthand knowledge. Even with the relentless press exposure and rumors, I never once read of a nasty or sarcastic remark attributed to Diana. Certainly, I had never heard an unkind word from her in our conversations or read one in her letters.

Diana seemed to be having every bit as difficult a time on her own as I'd feared. The constant, intrusive presence of the press could only be adding to her stress level. Even at the worst, she had only shown occasional poor judgment in her personal relationships. Diana had been so very innocent and inexperienced when she married, it is not surprising that she made mistakes once she was on her own. I wondered what the truth was about the strange phone calls to Oliver Hoare, the art dealer, or the rumors about Will Carling, the English rugby player. I was disappointed in her for the James Hewitt business, but the only person hurt in that situation was Diana herself. It is a shame that these incidents became so public. She seemed so vulnerable—her wealth and fame no shield from common hurts and betrayals.

I desperately wanted to see her again and have a heart-to-heart talk, but with Pat still in Asia, I could not leave my children for even a quick trip to London. I read about her spending one Christmas alone at Kensington Palace, waiting for her sons to return the next day for a trip with her to the Caribbean. I was appalled. Christmas alone? Where were her family and friends? I was deeply worried about her. The only thing I could do was to send another letter.

I continued to write to Diana from time to time with our

latest address changes, family news, and our constant affection for her. I remembered her plea from so long ago, "Please never stop writing . . ." Diana responded with her lovely Christmas cards and her warm, handwritten greetings—maybe her way of saying, "I remember." When I thought about it, I realized that I, too, have kept in touch with far-away friends through our Christmas cards. I miss these friends and would love to see them, but we are all so busy with our own lives that we just don't take the time to write or even call. In particularly stressful years, I don't even manage to send Christmas cards. Given the difficult time I knew Diana was having, it came as no surprise to me that she no longer wrote long, personal letters.

Diana's staff kept careful track of all our moves and address changes. Every year we received her Christmas card, always signed with love and sometimes the hugs and kisses symbols. After her separation, the photograph varied from year to year. In 1992, as I've said, the picture was of the boys looking rather lonely. For the next three years, her card showed Diana in a happy, intimate pose with her sons. In 1995, Diana wrote to me as "Mary" instead of "Mrs. Robertson" for the first time. That fall, a close friend, Janet Gaffney, had hand-delivered a short letter from me at Kensington Palace. In 1996 after her divorce, her card had a delightfully casual photograph, showing her boys with two smiling girl cousins on a tropical beach.

Each December I looked forward to receiving Diana's

Christmas card. I felt such joy when the mailman hand delivered the distinctive, stiff, formal envelope every year. Many years Diana sent Patrick his own card. We were probably the happiest recipients of Diana's Christmas cards anywhere in the world. I always placed her card on our mantel with the Christmas decorations and stockings. I'd leave it there for weeks, then put it in our bank deposit box for safekeeping. Diana's Christmas cards and letters will be family treasures for generations to come.

In 1997, there was no Christmas card from Diana. I cried inside when I looked at the empty spot on the mantel. I can still barely accept that Diana is gone. I'd planned to write again last September, telling her that Patrick was now in college and that we were coming to London next year, in the summer of 1998.

For Diana, there would be no 1998.

C H A P T E R

13

My seven-hour flight to London to attend Diana's funeral landed at ten o'clock Friday night. I'd been too tense to nap or eat on the airplane. Some of the cabin crew knew of my connection with Diana and expressed their sympathy, as well as their own sense of loss. The entire crew wanted to go into London to stand along the procession route and watch the funeral broadcast in Hyde Park, but their schedules would not allow it. The flight attendants mentioned an American couple on the flight who were traveling to London just to watch the procession and to hear the ceremony from the streets, along with the millions already in London. It was heartwarming to see firsthand what diverse lives Diana had touched.

As soon as we landed, I was stunned to learn that

Mother Teresa had died just hours earlier. It seemed incredible that the two most loved and admired women on earth had died within a week of each other. This was simply too much sorrow in too short a time.

As arranged, Floyd Bradley was waiting at Gatwick Airport to drive me to their home in Chelsea. It was such a comfort to see his calm, familiar face after my long, memory-filled trip. I was so frazzled that when we reached Floyd's car, I stood motionless by the right-hand door even after Floyd had walked around to the left door and held it open for me. He kept saying, "Wrong door, Mary. Wrong door." I couldn't even grasp what he was saying. I was so upset and distracted that I'd forgotten that the driver sits on the right in England.

As we drove toward London in the dark, Floyd told me that the public outpouring of grief had been overwhelming and unprecedented. People had waited in line at Saint James's Palace for hours just to sign the books of condolence. The public was not permitted to view the closed casket inside the palace. Floyd said normal activity in London had slowed to a crawl that week.

Diana's body had been moved to Kensington Palace the night before. The crowds had gathered there to pay tribute. Floyd said, "If you aren't too tired, you really ought to see for yourself how people are responding. It's unbelievable." Heavy traffic clogged the streets in Kensington even at twelve o'clock on that warm, clear night. We had to park blocks away from the palace and dodge our way through the crowds milling aimlessly on the sidewalks of the main streets. A sense of loss and helplessness showed on every face. People didn't seem to know where to go or what to do.

Floyd and I came first to the redbrick gates marked "Private Road" that led to the driveway our family had taken so cheerfully that sunny June day five years earlier. On Friday night, the gates were closed, guarded by policemen, and banked with hundreds of bouquets and messages. I blinked back tears and shuddered at the contrast.

The London bobbies were politely directing mourners toward an entrance to Kensington Gardens that lay several hundred yards past the driveway. Floyd and I walked in awed silence along the park fence, which had flowers, letters, photos, and stuffed animals wedged between every inch of the railings and piled up along the sidewalk. I agreed with Floyd: "This *is* unbelievable." The sidewalk was dimly lit by old-fashioned streetlamps. Cars crawled by slowly as drivers and passengers peered at the overflow of floral tributes.

Once inside the park, people followed a one-way traffic flow toward the "ocean" of flowers spreading across more than an acre in front of the formal black iron gates of the palace, which stood in almost total darkness. At this hour of the night, the throngs were mainly adults, but they were of all ages and races. In the dark, I couldn't tell if there were hundreds and hundreds of mourners or thousands and thousands. I was moved by how subdued and respectful everyone was. I could hear quiet sobbing and low voices expressing grief and sympathy. There was no need for crowd control, even though the crowd was so dense that I was afraid Floyd and I would get separated in the dark.

He and I gradually moved up toward the metal barriers delineating the front edge of the flood of bouquets. A handful of bobbies stood behind the fencing to receive the bouquets or other tributes from the individuals closest to them. They would then respectfully place each gift in the front row, which was creeping steadily forward. Floyd handed a waiting bobby his family's bouquet of deep red roses and letters from him and Amanda, his wife. As Floyd and I gazed at this overwhelming demonstration of love for Diana, we raised our eyes to the blank façade of Kensington Palace, Diana's former home.

Not a single lamp shone out from the windows into the darkness. The palace stood silent and empty. Two floodlights, set under the eaves, partially lit the façade. In the very center, Floyd and I noticed a faint eerie glow behind a row of windows on the top floor. Floyd turned to me: "Do you suppose that's where they placed her coffin?" I gazed up at the dimly lit windows and pictured Diana lying there in her coffin—cold, alone, dead.

My eyes filled with tears. I felt very cold. My heart was a lead weight in my chest. I looked at Floyd standing next to me. "I'm afraid so. My God, this is awful." We stood in silence a few moments longer. I could have stayed there all night, staring at those ghostly windows and grieving for Diana, but the people behind us needed their turn at the barrier.

Slowly, Floyd and I walked toward the street. We were reluctant to leave, even though it was after one o'clock by then. One final image struck us as we wandered out of the park. Circling every single tree at this end of the park were hundreds more bouquets, messages, pictures, and stuffed animals, all lit with countless flickering candles. Every tree had become a small shrine to Diana.

I'll never forget that night. The darkness, the hushed voices, the milling crowds, the acres of flowers and messages, the candlelit "shrines," and worst of all—the faintly lit windows indicating Diana's coffin in the dark. I would never have believed the depth of this public mourning if I hadn't seen it for myself. I was glad Floyd had insisted we come.

It seemed as if people were caught unawares by how much they had loved Diana. If you were there, you didn't just see the displays of affection and hear the sounds of grief, you could actually *feel* the love people were expressing for their princess.

The British people's astounding and heartfelt reaction was even more than shock and grief at Diana's death. It was a resounding, undeniable affirmation of Diana's intuitive, caring approach to people, of the new path she'd chosen.

As men and women quietly placed their bouquets and poems and wiped their tears, their message was clear and compelling. They loved Diana and pledged to remember her. Their testimony was all the more eloquent for its simplicity and silence.

*A*t seven the next morning I awoke in the Bradleys' guest room to a warm, clear, fall day. A cold drizzle would have matched my mood more closely. I felt utterly miserable, tired, and sad. I didn't know how I was going to cope with the anguish of the funeral on my own. This was probably going to be the most wrenching day of my life. A hot bath, two migraine pills, and a breakfast tray of fresh coffee and croissants from Amanda at least got me on my feet and out the door.

Floyd and I drove toward Westminster Abbey through totally deserted side streets to avoid the crowded route of Diana's cortege. Every person in London was either lined up outdoors to watch the funeral procession or viewing the event indoors on television. The Lord Chamberlain's office had instructed me to drive toward the Abbey until I came to a police blockade. At that point, the police would be "happy to give further assistance." Floyd and I were stopped at the corner of Millbank and Lambeth Bridge, where I had to show my black-edged admission ticket. Floyd gave me a good-luck hug. I turned to walk the remaining quarter mile along the Thames to Westminster Abbey.

I walked in the dappled sunlight under the trees with my thoughts in turmoil. It seemed impossible that on this beautiful sunny morning two thousand people were converging on the Abbey to say good-bye to an extraordinary young woman who'd been full of life and joy only a week before, in the prime of her life. She'd never had the happiness she deserved. She was too young to die. How could this have happened?

As I drew closer to the Abbey, I was asked again to show my admission ticket. My entrance was the Great North Door. Well before nine-thirty, when the Abbey doors were opened, a long line of mourners already wound from the gate outside the north door and around the corner. I took my place in line and looked around. Parliament Square and the nearby streets were packed. Mourners stood quietly and respectfully, dozens deep behind temporary barriers. Many were wearing dark clothing, black armbands, or ribbons. All were united in their need to express and share their grief. These spectators were confined to the opposite sides of the streets and the square from the Abbey. There were no empty spaces to be found. Only those with tickets were allowed on the sidewalk surrounding the Abbey and Saint Margaret's. If I hadn't seen the crowds the night before, I wouldn't have believed the masses and masses of people around the Abbey that morning. We were all very subdued.

A pretty young woman behind me asked, in a pleasantly accented voice, "What was your connection with the Princess of Wales?" I explained who I was and she introduced herself. I cannot recall her name, but she had been Diana's personal shopper at Selfridge's, a large London department store. She introduced me to her companion, Madame Ferragamo, from Italy. Then she explained to Madame Ferragamo in rapid Italian who I was. I heard the words, "madre," "bambino," "Americano." Madame Ferragamo spoke perfect English. I pointed to the black Ferragamo pumps I was wearing and told her that I'd worn them to lunch with Diana a few years ago. She seemed delighted that her family product had been so useful. She'd thought Diana was marvelous and regretted that she'd never met her. Then the two women switched back to Italian and I was on my own. Everyone else waiting to enter the church had a companion. I wished that Pat and my children had been able to come.

As I approached the Great North Door, I spied an attractive woman about my age standing by herself. I took a few paces forward to catch up with her and said, "We seem to be the only people here on our own. What was your connection with the Princess of Wales?" We struck up a conversation, introducing ourselves and explaining our respective positions here among the mourners. Out of respect for her privacy, I cannot divulge her identity, other than to say she was well connected in society. Nor is her identity essential to what follows.

My next question was, "Did you hear the queen's speech last night? I was on an airplane, so I missed it. What did you think?"

"Yes, and I didn't believe a word of it!" my new acquaintance answered emphatically.

I knew I'd found a kindred spirit. I hadn't heard the Queen's address, but I'd read it in the paper early that morning. I ventured my opinion that the carefully worded speech had been "too little, too late." Along with most of the British press and public, I'd been baffled by the royal family's failure to express regret about Diana's death for almost a week. Surely a few timely and heartfelt sentences from Balmoral would not have interfered with the family's first priority—to protect and comfort Diana's sons.

Once inside the cathedral, I was surprised that the seating was first come, first served, not assigned, as it had been at the wedding. The explanation was obvious—the wedding had been planned for months; the funeral, for only a few days. There were virtually no empty seats remaining in the unreserved section. I wished I'd arrived much earlier.

The only face I recognized among those already seated in the north transept was Ralph Lauren, the American designer, with his wife.

As my new acquaintance and I walked up the aisle under the soaring Gothic arches, she raised her eyes heavenward and fervently wished aloud, "Diana, I hope you can see all this."

"Yes," I thought, "please, God, let Diana see the cathedral filled to overflowing with mourners from all walks of life. And even more, the millions of ordinary people all over England and the world. Please, let her know how truly loved she was."

The steward who was directing us headed toward a side aisle between the choir stalls and the outer wall. From there, we wouldn't be able to see a thing at the front of the church directly, only on the television monitor set up for this remote location. My heart sank.

Luckily, my companion was more quick-witted than I. She spotted two empty seats at the very front in the unreserved section and next to the press section. We plunked ourselves down immediately and firmly, ignoring the steward who was kind enough to leave us where we were. From this location at the corner of the north transept, we had a clear view of the front of the nave, where the clergy and most speakers would stand, and the pulpit on our side, from which Diana's brother would later speak. We could just glimpse the far lectern where Tony Blair would read.

Twenty feet in front of us was a large television monitor, so we could view the parts of the ceremony we could not actually see. We felt very fortunate with our location, especially given our relatively late arrival. Our only problem now was the shortage of programs. My friend asked an usher for at least one program for "this lady who has come all the way from America." Her plea fell on deaf ears. The man hissed crankily at us that we'd get our programs, when and if more were available.

Next I overheard a dignified, gray-haired steward, who was surveying the dwindling supply of seats and programs, say in a baffled voice, "We weren't expecting so many people." Did they really expect anyone would turn down the privilege of attending Diana's funeral?

By ten-fifteen, our section of the Abbey was filled. The north transept is the left arm of the cross-shaped cathedral. It is known as Statesmen's Aisle for the many statues of England's political leaders placed there. The lantern or crossing of the church was reserved for the royal family, the Spencer family, close relatives and friends of both families, and, after eleven o'clock, for Diana's casket. The more famous guests, the celebrities and politicians, were seated facing the center aisle in the nave, the long main body of the Abbey. Their view of the ceremony, which would take place at the front of the nave, was severely restricted by the ornate, carved choir screen, which stretched across the nave with an opening only in the center. However, the most illustrious attendees as well as the royal and Spencer families would process up and then back down the center aisle. My new friend and I would have a better view of the ceremony, but we would have to watch the procession on the monitor.

The morning sunlight filtered softly through the translucent, mullioned windows of the transept, set in their graceful Gothic arches. We could hear muffled bells, way up in the tower, tolling mournfully at one-minute intervals to mark Diana's four-mile journey from Kensington Palace. Stately organ music by Bach and Pachelbel, Elgar and Vaughan Williams, filled the cool, gray vaulted spaces of England's most historic cathedral. The congregation around us was largely silent, as we waited in somber anticipation.

I felt so wretched to be at Diana's funeral that I couldn't summon up even a faint memory of the joy we'd felt at her wedding in a different cathedral sixteen years ago. I wondered how many others in the congregation had known the young Diana and attended her wedding. She had been a happy, uncomplicated teenager when I first knew her. Now she had died, complex and fascinating, the most famous woman on earth. On the surface, she'd possessed everything one could wish for—beauty, wealth, and fame—but these gifts had never brought her happiness, or even peace of mind. I marveled at the extraordinary human being she'd become—transformed by her personal crises into an icon the world would love and revere, always, for her compassion, her vulnerability, and her honesty.

Along with my crushing sorrow, I felt tremendous anger, even though I knew it was uncharitable of me. The whole world was mourning a tragic death in a senseless car accident that should have been prevented. If her personal situation had been different, she wouldn't have been in that car in the first place, and she wouldn't have died. I blamed everyone who hadn't given her the support and love she needed when she was so young and innocent. How could those closest to her have missed or ignored her legitimate problems, her obvious vulnerability? I could respect their grief and remorse now, but I was still angry.

What I could not begin to fathom was the heartbreak and desolation her sons must be feeling, now and for so long a time to come. I pondered her untimely death and grieved for her motherless sons.

My new acquaintance had known Diana in recent years. There was so much I wanted to know. I explained I'd known Diana well as a young woman and had loved her warm, gentle, and unassuming qualities. Had she changed? My friend assured me that she had not, but she had grown up and matured considerably. She emphasized that Diana would have wanted to be remembered for her "courage, compassion, and intelligence."

My companion had recently lunched with Diana at Kensington Palace. She said being with Diana was like "being brushed by angels' wings." I loved that phrase and will remember it always. I knew exactly what she meant.

Diana's presence had a graceful, gentle, magical quality.

I was intrigued to learn that Diana had developed "a rather mutinous streak." If she was told that a proposed mission was dangerous, she became even more determined to go. An example of this had been her recent trip to Angola to visit land mine victims.

This marvelous woman sitting next to me had clearly loved and admired Diana as I had. It was such a comfort to share our memories. I was glad to know that Diana had sought the friendship of remarkable women like this—intelligent, sensitive, experienced in the ways of the world, successful in their own careers. Diana had needed such friends to give her wise and sensible advice as she had defined her new life. I only wished she'd known them earlier.

We watched on the television monitor as such world-famous guests as Hillary Clinton, Luciano Pavarotti, Margaret Thatcher, Tom Cruise and Nicole Kidman, and other entertainment figures entered the nave. We heard a collective sigh of sympathy as Mohammed Al Fayed, Dodi's father, took his place in the congregation. My friend identified the peripheral members of the royal family as they advanced up the center aisle. Ahead of us in the north transept, we recognized Diana's stepmother, Raine, striking in a black-and-white flowered outfit that my companion observed would be "more suited to a garden party than a funeral."

It was just minutes before eleven o'clock. The Spencer

family and the Queen, the Queen Mother, and the families of Princess Margaret, Princess Anne, and Prince Andrew with his family had arrived at their places under the crossing. The congregation sat subdued and pensive. There was very little conversation as we waited. Most people appeared lost in their own thoughts. Others perused the programs we had all finally received. The somber blacks and blues and grays worn by men and women alike served as a fitting background to all of our solemn thoughts. This was an unmitigated tragedy. We were grieving together.

We had seen occasional distant views of the cortege on the monitor screen. By now, we knew, Diana's cortege was nearing the Abbey, completing its long, sad journey through streets banked by mourners. We knew Diana's young sons, accompanied by their father, uncle, and grandfather, had been following her coffin from Saint James's Palace.

I dreaded the moment when Diana's coffin would inevitably appear. My heart began to pound and my pulse to race. I was in the grip of completely overpowering emotion, but I still didn't expect the visceral impact my first view of her coffin on the monitor would produce.

Diana's solitary, draped casket, drawn upon a gun carriage, halted outside the Great West Door. The impact of her physical presence among us was heart-stopping. Total silence fell over the congregation.

I gasped, "Oh, no," and held my breath. Tears streamed down my cheeks. Icy chills ran down my back.

Diana's casket was so powerful and evocative a symbol of her loneliness and vulnerability, I could hardly bear to look at it. My companion reached over and gently squeezed my hand to comfort and to sympathize.

Eight Welsh Guards carried Diana's coffin slowly up the center aisle. From our seats we could see only the front end of the casket. We could not see the members of the royal family, who were seated on the far side of the coffin. To my left, I observed rows of journalists busily writing notes for their papers and magazines.

Diana's funeral was a profoundly moving and uplifting farewell to a unique and greatly loved young woman. More than two billion people watched the ceremony only a few months ago, so I will describe only my own reactions and impressions from that unforgettable hour.

I still don't understand why, but my heart continued to race for the next hour. At particularly touching moments in the prayers or music, I would find I'd been holding my breath without realizing it. I loved Diana's favorite hymn from her youth, "I Vow to Thee, My Country," Elton John's affecting song, and her brother's spellbinding tribute. After the initial shock of seeing her coffin, I didn't cry openly again. Rather, I sat overwhelmed by sorrow for the next hour, wiping at the tears behind my glasses with one of Pat's large handkerchiefs I'd brought along. During the first prayer, I felt a searing pain in my chest and thought, "It's true. You can actually feel your heart breaking." I experienced another particularly bad moment when the monitor displayed a dramatic view from 150 feet up in the lantern, directly down upon Diana's casket. Her red-and-gold-draped coffin looked so small and lost, adrift on the vast expanse of the black-and-white-checkered floor. It was a mesmerizing image.

I was intrigued to note, at the very start of the ceremony, that more than one person near me did not join in England's national anthem, "God Save the Queen." Whether this was a quiet protest against the royal family's muted response to Diana's death, I couldn't tell. As the anthem began, I overheard one person mutter, "May she drop dead tomorrow!" I didn't sing—it wasn't my national anthem.

Throughout the service, I kept thinking, again and again, "None of us should even be here. Diana never should have died." Here we were—thousands in the Abbey, a million on London's streets—mourning a death that never should have happened. I still can't bear the thought of Diana's death even now, months later.

Prime Minister Tony Blair read the famous verses about faith, hope, and love from Paul's First Letter to the Corinthians that I'd heard at Diana's wedding. His voice rang with emotion and conviction. I knew he had greatly admired Diana. The final phrase, "And now abideth faith, hope, love, these three; but the greatest of these is love," carried tragic relevance that day. Diana was all about love.

A marvelous, unexpected moment occurred immediately after Elton John's heartfelt song for "England's rose." Those of us inside the Abbey heard a rustling, pattering sound coming from outside. We all thought rain had started to fall. All heads turned toward the windows to look. The sun was still shining. My friend murmured, "They're clapping outside." Then the entire congregation realized what we'd just heard was spontaneous applause from the crowds listening to the loudspeakers outside the Abbey. I hadn't realized before that the service was being broadcast to the thousands outside who wanted to participate in this farewell to Diana. The public wanted its support for Diana to be heard, loud and clear, by those inside the church.

Next, the Earl Spencer's speech held us all spellbound. His address was conspicuously the only section of the service not already printed in the program. We should have known it would be remarkable. And it was—eloquent, passionate, unforgettable. I held my breath as I listened.

I would not have altered a syllable of the words he spoke in praise of his "extraordinary" sister. I especially loved his affirmation of her appeal to millions who'd never met her, her compassion, her "natural nobility," her "genuine goodness." I was relieved to hear him declare that "fundamentally she hadn't changed at all" and had "remained intact, true to herself." This was what I had always believed of Diana. We could see he was choking with emotion as he concluded his tribute.

For the second time that morning, we heard the sound

of rain pattering. This time we recognized it instantly as applause from the crowds outside. The sound swept through the Abbey. Tentatively at first, then wholeheartedly, the congregation's applause erupted in overwhelming support of the Earl's praise of his beloved sister.

My companion whispered, "It's unheard of to clap in church in England. It's never been done before." This heartfelt and unprecedented response to her brother's tribute was undoubtedly the most stirring moment of the service. My newfound friend and I clapped long and hard. The Earl had clearly wanted to make an impact with his remarks, and he most assuredly did.

This spontaneous outburst was followed by the touching and simple hymn, "Make Me a Channel of Your Peace," with words by Saint Francis of Assisi. Its calm and sincere message seemed particularly beautiful and fitting at this point in the service. Then the service proceeded smoothly with eloquent prayers by the Archbishop of Canterbury and The Lord's Prayer, interspersed with hymns. During the final hymn from the choir, the lyrical solo phrase "Remember me, O Lord" floated high above the voices of the choir. The congregation rose as the Welsh Guards shouldered Diana's casket and carried their precious burden back through the nave. Softly, the last notes of the hymn faded into the air.

In that brief moment of silence, the stately, measured tread of the guards' boots echoed, hollow against the soaring stone vaults and columns. Those footsteps sounded so stark, so final. Diana was leaving . . . forever. I held my breath, rigid with emotion. For my part, this was the most heartbreaking moment of the entire funeral.

At the west end of the church, the guards paused with Diana's casket for a full minute of silence, which was honored all across Great Britain. The Dean of Westminster stood silhouetted against the sunlit Great West Door, facing Diana's coffin. It seemed as if all time had stopped. That incredible silence, then the muffled bells of the Abbey rang out again.

The Windsors, the Spencers, and the clergy departed back through the nave, following the path of the casket. We were asked to remain in our seats until the stewards invited us to leave. After the overpowering emotions the funeral had evoked, I was relieved to sit quietly to pull myself together. My companion kindly offered me a ride back to Chelsea, but I had agreed to do a brief interview right after the ceremony. We waved our programs triumphantly at the usher who'd been so snappy to us earlier. He smiled back, relieved that the pressure of the funeral was over.

Before we left the Abbey, my new friend and I paused in the now deserted transept. She told me the most poignant story about the last time she'd seen Diana a few weeks earlier, just after the memorial service for Gianni Versace, the Italian fashion designer who had been killed. Diana had said that she believed the point of a memorial service was to celebrate the life of the person, once the mourning period was over. She found that it was difficult to stop grieving for a young person, like Versace, who'd been cut down in his prime. The irony of Diana's observation so soon before her own untimely death was bitter. My companion and I knew neither of us would stop grieving for Diana for a long, long time.

Before we parted, she and I exchanged telephone numbers and have spoken since. I may never see that marvelous woman again, but I'll never forget her. She was amazing in her own right—intelligent, witty, successful, kind. And we had shared a heartbreaking, once-in-a-lifetime experience that morning. I paused on the lawn at the north side of the Abbey for a final reflection.

Attending Diana's funeral was the saddest thing I've ever done. The image of her solitary coffin and the haunting echo of the guards' footsteps will stay with me always. I prayed for her young sons, for whom she will be irreplaceable.

I looked across the square at the thousands of people who remained, listening to the Abbey bells, unwilling to leave. Men and women alike were still blinking back tears, biting trembling lips, or openly crying after seeing Diana's casket being borne away.

The funeral service had been truly sublime—a funeral fit for a queen. Yet, Diana would have been more deeply touched by the unprecedented and heartfelt expressions of love and loss from ordinary people. She had said she wanted to be a "princess for the world." The world's sorrow for her untimely death made it undeniably clear that she was, indeed, "the people's princess," as Tony Blair had so eloquently called her. On that mournful day, her lonely path away from royal convention had been completely vindicated.

But the cost had been too high.

∞

O n my way back to Chelsea
that afternoon, I stopped at
Eaton Mews South with the ABC news crew, so I could
show them where we'd lived in 1980—the street where
Diana had first walked out with Patrick to face the press. I
recognized the neighbors' houses and the shops nearby. It
seemed like only yesterday. Now Patrick was busy at college, and Diana had died. The unfairness of it all overwhelmed me.

Back at the Bradleys', Floyd was watching a videotape of
the funeral, since he'd been standing along the cortege route
at the time of the ceremony. I was exhausted. A glass of club
soda was shaking in my hand. I was feeling so fragile, I didn't
dare risk a real drink. Floyd and I sat on the sofa in their family room, the doors open to their leafy, green, walled garden.

On the tape, I saw what I had not been able to see at the Abbey—the wreath of white roses on top of Diana's coffin bearing the envelope addressed to "Mummy" in Prince Harry's handwriting. I thought that note was the most touching, poignant image of the entire day.

I remembered the enchanting child we'd met at Kensington Palace and how absolutely Diana had loved her boys. I couldn't begin to imagine Harry's feelings—despair, bewilderment, loss—as he wrote "Mummy" for the last time. I wandered out into the garden as evening fell to cry softly by myself.

Weeks before, Floyd and Amanda had planned an evening out with friends visiting from Sweden. Floyd had made reservations at San Lorenzo, Diana's favorite restaurant. I wasn't feeling very sociable, but I didn't want to appear ungrateful for the invitation to join them. We had a relaxing dinner and discussed a wide range of topics. But the conversation did, inevitably, return time and again to Diana and her extraordinary appeal. We avoided talking about her death, as I was clearly still overwrought. In fact, I was so tired I could barely chew. I ordered risotto for dinner and zabaglione, a soft custard, for dessert. The Bradleys teased me gently about ordering "nursery food" for supper. We were home by midnight, just before I would have collapsed.

Sunday morning I woke up at seven. I had another migraine, took two pills, and waited for the pain to go away. I propped myself up against the soft, white, embroidered pillows and wrapped the snowy down comforter around me. I was looking forward to a day to myself, now that the ordeal of the funeral was over. I sat huddled on the bed, staring at the blue-and-white-curtained window ahead of me. Then I began to sob and sob and sob about Diana's death. It was such a relief to vent the grief that I'd kept bottled up inside for a week. Now, for the first time, I had an insight as to why Diana had stayed in touch with us for so long. I'd never questioned it before, but news reporters and interviewers had often asked me about it.

We were not a part of her new life. We could do nothing for her, but we asked nothing of her, either—only friendship from Diana herself, not as the Princess of Wales. I had made that point very clear in my letters. I hoped she'd seen them. We had always offered her unstinting admiration, support, and love. She must have remembered that we had accepted her in our home and trusted her with our child when she was "nobody," as she had said. We had not even known she was an aristocratic nobody. She had been very happy the year she took care of Patrick and had told me the memories meant a great deal to her.

As she grew older and became a mother herself, she probably remembered how she had "adored" Patrick as a baby. She understood how devoted I was to my son, then my daughter, now that she was devoted to her own boys. We both knew that children need love and support, bedtime stories and hugs. It was this mother-to-mother bond that we shared. At lunch five years ago, she'd said of her children, "They're my life," and I'd agreed with all my heart.

Sunday afternoon Floyd wanted to show his young children, Camilla, William, and Melissa, the display of flowers and messages at Kensington Palace. Thousands of people were still streaming toward the palace to look at the ocean of bouquets and messages or to leave their own. Hundreds of others stood in line on the opposite side of the palace to sign the books of condolence. I couldn't believe the vast numbers of people still paying tribute to their princess.

The day was warm and sunny, so the palace and the masses of flowers looked very different from Friday night. The feeling of the crowd had also changed. Now that the ritual of the funeral was over, people were remembering Diana's life and accomplishments and how much they loved her. The funeral service had produced closure for many people.

The crowds were as dense as they had been on Friday night. I was concerned about losing track of the children. I had only two hands, and Floyd was striding ahead of the four of us. Floyd had to lift his children onto his shoulders so they could see over the heads of those closer to the barrier where he and I had stood Friday night. We couldn't locate the Bradleys' bouquet, so many had been added since then. I was relieved to see the palace in the sunlight and to know Diana's coffin was no longer resting inside.

In the midst of this milling throng, a petite young brunette, a complete stranger, turned to me: "Did you ever meet the Princess of Wales?" I think she was surprised when I told her how well I'd known Diana. She was eager to tell me of her secondhand experience with Diana. A close friend of hers had a young child whom Diana had met at one of the hospitals she supported. Diana had sent birthday cards to the youngster "every year. She never forgot. It was amazing how kind she was," the young woman concluded. I agreed wholeheartedly. When I told Floyd about the encounter, he observed that even if a fine and efficient staff had arranged to send the cards, Diana had been the one to "make it happen."

I needed that sunny afternoon with Floyd's children, playing catch by the Duck Pond and climbing at the playground, to balance the gloom of the previous few days. As the children and I wandered in the park, we noticed a letter pinned to a small tree, set off by itself. That week, the London papers had reported that all the messages and letters and poems would be saved for Diana's family to read, over time. I wondered if this message, far from the palace, would be overlooked. I read it aloud to Floyd's children. Later reports said the thousands of messages would be shredded.

One phrase seemed particularly apt. The writer described the "carpet of flowers to mark her progress. This would have touched her soul, as she touched ours." I loved the image of Diana touching people's *souls*. Diana *did* touch people—their faces and hands, their hearts and souls. She expressed her love and concern in a visible, tactile way that everyone could feel and understand.

I thought of the CBS Skytel reporter who'd surprised me on my driveway the week before the funeral. He'd asked me what *single* word or image I would choose to describe Diana. I blurted out "hugs" without even thinking. My sense of Diana as a loving, touching person was that deeply ingrained.

Late Monday night, I experienced a heartwarming moment after appearing on CNN's *Larry King Live*. When my segment of the show ended at two thirty, I walked downstairs with Floyd, who'd stayed up half the night to keep me company. We found Hugo Vickers, a royal biographer and fellow guest, waiting for me in the entrance hall. With a warm smile, he said, "May I please ask, what is that lucky little boy doing now?" I thought he had been very balanced and fair on the show. I liked him and was touched by his evidently sincere interest. I told him that my son, Patrick, was now eighteen and had just entered an Ivy League college.

I added, "Patrick shares one wonderful quality with Prince William. He is very protective of his mother." On that warm and tender note, we parted. My television "career" was over, and not a minute too soon.

In London, as I waited around broadcasting sets and

walked through the crowds at Kensington Palace and Westminster Abbey, I overheard bits of conversation that I found fascinating.

Given that many of the people around me worked in the media, a major topic was Diana's ambivalent attitude toward the press. Diana would be happy to accommodate the press when it suited her, either to express a private point of view or to publicize her charity efforts. She hated the press when they were intrusive in her personal life. The feeling expressed by the television people was that she couldn't have it both ways. In fact, there was an implication that the paparazzi's alleged role in Diana's fatal accident should not have been a surprise. I thought this apparent lack of understanding for Diana's ongoing dilemma vis-à-vis the press was unthinking and unkind. To be fair, if it hadn't been for the unrelenting press coverage, the world would never have known Diana and loved her and mourned her so profoundly.

I overheard two men talking about the terrible loss for Diana's sons. One voiced the opinion that they would recover in time: "After all, they're almost grown men now." No mother would ever describe boys of thirteen and fifteen as "grown men." I did not turn around, but I was tempted to object strenuously. In their early teens, most young men still feel unsure and vulnerable—very much in need of the unconditional love and support a mother like Diana would give.

My favorite remark was from a woman. "She never had

a happy moment once *they* [meaning the royal family] got their hooks into her." This was very sad and very true, but the phrasing and the wry tone of voice struck me as amusing when I heard it.

I overheard one telling comment about Diana's sisters: "Sarah's been an absolute rock through all this," followed by, "and, of course, Jane hasn't spoken to her since that television interview." This surprised me. Diana had been closer to Lady Jane in 1980 when Diana had taken Patrick to her sister's home in London and had visited her in Scotland. I was glad to hear that Diana and Lady Sarah had become closer in recent years. Diana had needed people she could trust. I was appalled that Lady Jane would not have supported her own sister, but I could imagine that, because of her connection with the palace, she had felt torn between the two sides of the bitter and public rift between the Prince and Princess of Wales.

Another time I heard that Diana and her ex-husband had been getting along better than ever since the divorce. I hoped this was true. Although I truly liked what I'd seen of Prince Charles, I would have taken Diana's side any day. Still, many observers felt that Prince Charles had been a victim of his upbringing and position. He probably could not have behaved differently, given the emotional burdens he carried from his youth. I heard that he was devoted to his sons and would commit himself to filling the void in the boys' lives. I believe this completely.

I overheard someone commenting that Diana had been quite proud that the Spencers' aristocratic lineage went back generations further than the Windsors'. And, she was pleased that her sons had the Spencer looks and coloring, not the Windsor features. I heard the Spencer temper, or "fire," mentioned as one reason why Diana had refused to overlook her husband's relationship with another woman. I had never seen any sign of a temper in the year she had cared for my son.

There was unanimous agreement with Diana's view that the older members of the royal family were out of touch with the values and expectations of their subjects. They had proved it with their stifled behavior in the week following Diana's death. The Queen was viewed as largely irrelevant to a Britain entering the next millennium. Many people were beginning to feel tolerant and forgiving towards Prince Charles, willing to give him his chance to rule when the time comes. Mainly, though, the public's hopes for the future are firmly pinned on Diana's sons.

Everyone was so focused on Diana that I never heard a word about Dodi himself or his recent relationship with Diana, although people sympathized very sincerely with his father's loss.

By Tuesday, it was time for me to go home. On the way to the airport, our driver told us the crowds were still out in droves at Kensington Palace, with no end in sight. I was glad that public support for Diana was still so evident.

After the shattering events of the past ten days, I was happy to fly home and return to my normal, everyday life. Pat met me at the airport, then we picked up a very unhappy Caroline after school. She'd been missing Patrick desperately since he'd left for college. In my short absence, she'd experienced an unexpectedly rough adjustment to her new high school. This had been a bad time for me to be away. She felt abandoned. Caroline burst into tears of relief the minute she stepped into the car. I just held her close for the twenty-minute ride home. We went straight up to her cozy pink bedroom to talk. She sobbed that she'd been miserable while I was away. "Daddy has been wonderful, but a daddy is not a mommy. I really needed you." I choked back my own tears. "But, Caroline, darling," I said, "I was only gone for five days. Just think of William and Harry. Their mummy is *never* coming back."

The reactions of our personal friends may reflect to a large degree Diana's worldwide and lasting appeal. We received letters and phone calls from friends living, literally, all over the world—Malaysia, Sumatra, Brazil, Australia, Europe, and throughout America—many of whom had not known of our connection with Diana until they saw me on television. The fact that so many of our far-flung and diverse friends were watching the television coverage of Diana's death and funeral spoke volumes in itself. They were shocked and saddened by Diana's death but acknowledged, "It must be so much worse for you. You knew her."

One comment I heard repeated by men and women friends alike, was, "I didn't really follow her that closely, so I was surprised at how upset I was by her death." Again, that undeniable and universal appeal.

Women friends, mothers my own age, referred to her so often as "that poor child." Incredible. Diana was beautiful, rich, the most famous woman of her era, yet what spoke to all of us was her vulnerability.

Some comparison with Jackie Kennedy Onassis was inevitable. Jackie had been the most famous woman of her day—an icon of beauty and style, a devoted mother, a private person hounded by the press. Diana had sought the protection and privacy Dodi could offer, just as Jackie had turned to Aristotle Onassis. Both Diana and Jackie came from the upper classes of their respective societies, born with poise and grace. The critical difference was that Diana possessed the common touch and genuine feeling for ordinary people that endeared her to millions.

Others likened Diana to Jack Kennedy. Both had died too soon and too suddenly, cut down in their prime, to be remembered always as youthful and vibrant. One dear friend consoled me by saying, "Remember, Mary, she'll always be thirty-six, young and beautiful." Another close friend wrote, "We'll never know what she's been spared."

Even after the funeral, the trips to Kensington Palace, and the consolation of friends, I still couldn't accept Diana's death. Then, Mr. Jeffrey Ling, the British consul general in

New York, invited me to speak at the memorial service for Diana in Central Park the weekend after the funeral. I was grateful for the chance to speak about Diana in my own words and at my own pace. Pat and I rewrote my three-minute speech over and over. I practiced it several times the night before.

On Sunday afternoon I visited backstage with Mr. Ling and Mayor Giuliani before the service began. The mayor was engaging and down to earth. Mr. Ling was gracious and reassuring, a true gentleman. We watched the North Meadow fill up with more than ten thousand people and were grateful to see such a big turnout on a hot, sunny day. As I sat on the stage, I grew more nervous by the minute. I delivered my heartfelt speech, trembling with emotion as I spoke about "the Diana we knew."

As I looked out at the crowded meadow, I pondered the incredible path I'd traveled, all because I'd needed a part-time nanny in London seventeen years ago. I'd enjoyed a remarkable friendship, attended the most famous cere-monies of my lifetime, dined and danced in palaces, visited with royalty—extraordinary experiences for me and my family.

Now, tragically, it was all ending here, as I spoke from my heart in memory and praise of my friend Diana.

∞

EPILOGUE

I miss Diana more than I can express. The world seems a colder place without her luminous presence. To had had Diana's friendship, to have known her personally, has been a gift beyond comparison. She brought joy and pride and a touch of glamour to my life for years. I loved and admired her without reservation.

When Patrick recognized her picture on magazine covers, I thought how incredible it was that we actually knew the beautiful, famous Diana. Best of all, we knew she was even lovelier inside. I read her letters, feeling deeply touched that she continued to care for us. Seeing her in person—warm, unpretentious, and radiant—was a thrill that lasted a long, long time. It truly was, "like being brushed by angels' wings," as my friend at the funeral had said.

Whoever would have thought when I called for a nanny so many years ago, that magic would enter my life.

My family and I watched her dazzling progress from a shy teenager to a multi-faceted and charismatic woman. She fulfilled her many roles so beautifully. Yet to me, Diana was a beloved friend, not the world-famous Princess of Wales. Behind the glamour, I saw the qualities I'd always admired in her—kindness, integrity, and grace in all she did.

Above all, Diana was born to be a mother. Showing affection was as natural to her as breathing. I saw her tender care for my young son. I know she was an utterly devoted mother to her own boys, giving them unconditional love and deriving her greatest joy in life from them.

I've wished so often that her life had been a fairytale, that Diana had been spared the pain and loneliness she suffered. But without the despair, she might not have developed the strength and humanity that reached out to people everywhere. Diana instinctively looked beyond her own problems to ease the pain and distress of others. She touched so many people in her short lifetime.

I never thought it would end this way—that she would die so young. I will always remember, as the last hymn faded into silence at her funeral, the solemn tread of the soldiers' boots—so haunting, so final—as they carried her casket through the Abbey. I couldn't bear that she was leaving forever.

For months now, I've searched for some solace in this

tragedy. I hope that Diana's untimely death and the world-wide mourning for her have silenced forever those who belittled her values and doubted her appeal. She rests peacefully now beyond reproach—young and beautiful.

Diana, you were greater than we realized.

We will never, never forget you.

May 13th 1982.

Dear Mrs Robertson,

What a co...
surprise to find such a ...
newsy letter waiting f...
me — Please never stop writ...
as I always remember ...
with fondness & look forwa...
to hearing how ...

I miss Pa...
but hope t...
...dshe...
...t too...
...o its...
...s t...
...ave so...
...s woma...
...uch that e...
right sou...
lots of...

KENSINGTON PALACE

January: 25th
1987.

as w... Dearest Patrick,
...ch an... It was so ve...
This comes with...
big thank you &...
huge hug,

& as always
lots of love from

Diana. ⊕   for
hope

Mrs Cha...
of Patrick ...
...sh't wa...
...nuisance...
...w ms...
...t Parm...
since I'm ...
about him